REVOLUTIONARY HEBREW, EMPIRE AND CRISIS

Also by David Aberbach

CHARISMA IN POLITICS, RELIGION AND THE MEDIA
Private Trauma, Public Ideals

IMPERIALISM AND BIBLICAL PROPHECY 750–500 BCE

SURVIVING TRAUMA: Loss, Literature and Psychoanalysis

Revolutionary Hebrew, Empire and Crisis

Four Peaks in Hebrew Literature and Jewish Survival

David Aberbach

Associate Professor of Hebrew and Comparative Literature
McGill University

and

Visiting Academic
Department of Sociology
London School of Economics and Political Science

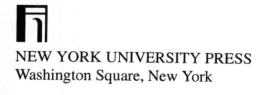

NEW YORK UNIVERSITY PRESS
Washington Square, New York

First published in the U.S.A. in 1998 by
NEW YORK UNIVERSITY PRESS
Washington Square
New York, N.Y. 10003

This book is printed on paper suitable for recycling and
made from fully managed and sustained forest sources.

Library of Congress Cataloging-in-Publication Data
Aberbach, David, 1953–
Revolutionary Hebrew, empire, and crisis : four peaks in Hebrew
literature and Jewish survival / David Aberbach.
 p. cm.
Includes bibliographical references and index.
ISBN 0–8147–0673–8
1. Hebrew literature—History and criticism. 2. Hebrew
literature—Political aspects. 3. Politics and literature.
4. Literature and history. 5. Jews—History—Miscellanea.
I. Title.
PJ5010.A34 1997
892.4'09358—dc21   97–13467
                                                  CIP
                                                  r97

Printed in Great Britain

To my students and colleagues at McGill University, Montreal, with affectionate thanks

Contents

Preface and Acknowledgements

My grandparents were Hebrew teachers in Vienna before the Second World War. Their profession (though in truth many people at the time, including one Austrian police officer who interviewed my grandmother when her husband needed a work permit, denied that it was a profession) unexpectedly saved their lives. After the *Anschluss* of March 1938, my father was taken in a *Kindertransport* to Leeds. His fluent Hebrew so impressed local Jewish communal officials that they arranged for visas to be granted to both his parents. They arrived in England in the last spring before the war and for the rest of their lives worked as Hebrew teachers in Leeds and London. My father was the only one in his transport who managed to get his parents out.

This book owes much to my being a child of refugees and a consequent fascination with the language that for three thousand years has been instrumental in the survival of the Jews. My chief debt is to my father and grandmother who taught me Hebrew and gave me a lasting, at times perhaps excessive reverence for Hebrew literature and the power of language. Together they introduced me to three of the four bodies of Hebrew which figure in this book; I discovered medieval Hebrew poetry much later, by teaching it at McGill University.

Thinking back on the evolution of this book, it seems to me that its thesis came to me – I did not look for it – as I worked backward from the modern period. By teaching and writing books and articles on Hebrew literature of the 1881–1917 period, I became aware of the symbiotic, ambivalent bond between Hebrew and the empires in which it was written. Many of the most remarkable creative phases in the artistic growth of Hebrew literature coincided with moments of severe crisis, when the empires which controlled the majority of the world Jewish population had fallen, were threatened with collapse or potentially fatal weaknesses. My books on the two leading Hebrew writers of the 1881–1917 period, Mendele Mocher Sefarim and Chaim Nachman Bialik, show how closely the emergence of modern Hebrew art was linked with the decline of the Tsarist empire. These books are the basis of Chapter 4, and their

Acknowledgements apply here as well. Another book of mine, *Imperialism and Biblical Prophecy 750–500 BCE*, was a run-up to this book. Its contents are summarized and amplified in the Introduction and in Chapter 1. Again, its Acknowledgements apply here too.

The role of collective disaster and cultural expressions of grief is paramount in the interpretation of Hebrew literature in this book. Here, again, I draw on prior work, especially *Surviving Trauma: loss, literature and psychoanalysis*.

Specific social and political circumstances and events also underlie this book. I had relatively little understanding of the effect of dominant empires and their cultures on minorities before I came to McGill University, Montreal, in 1986. It is hardly possible to live in Quebec without becoming sharply, at times uncomfortably, aware of the political significance of language and culture. For several years I taught a course in Hebrew on 'Dynamic Themes in Hebrew Literature'. The aim of this course was to demonstrate the evolution of Hebrew literature in its four main periods – Bible, Talmud, the medieval 'golden age' and the modern period – through a close study of literary themes which recur in each period. This course became the practical basis of this book, which grew out of detailed analyses of Hebrew texts in relation to their religious, social and historical background. Gradually, I began to see patterns in the development of Hebrew as a minority culture under the rule of leading empires.

To the best of my knowledge, the approach of this book and the sum of its conclusions have no precedent in the literature on Hebrew.

The genesis of this book was greatly affected, too, by the collapse of the Soviet empire and the emergence of many suppressed nationalisms from its ruins after 1989. Jewish cultural nationalism, whose chief instrument was Hebrew, could be seen as an antecedent of this revolution. For Hebrew is the classical expression of minority cultural nationalism under the rule of a dominant empire. The biblical prophets may be seen as archetypal literary dissidents.

These ideas drew me to the London School of Economics, where the study of nationalism, both current and historical, is a major area of research and teaching. Since 1992 I have been an Academic Visitor in the Sociology Department at the LSE, and it was there that the bulk of the book was written.

The parameters of the book are defined and justified in the Introduction, but brief mention of some of its limits may be helpful here. This book is not a comprehensive history of Hebrew literature. It does not aim to establish a 'scientific' symmetry between Hebrew literature and the vicissitudes of empires. Rather, it is an admittedly controversial interpretative essay. It tries to throw light on the nature of minority creativity on a broad social and political canvas. Its general aim is to show that Hebrew literature in several of its most original and revolutionary periods prior to 1948 did not come into being in a political and cultural vacuum but is itself evidence of a dynamic relationship with the dominant empires in which it was written. The idea of 'revolutionary' Hebrew does not refer to technical or generic breakthroughs, for example the introduction of Arabic versification in Hebrew poetry in the 10th century or the creation of the Hebrew novel in the 19th century. Instead, it refers to bodies of Hebrew literature which, by common critical agreement, have had revolutionary influence and lasting value as art. As this book is concerned with Hebrew literature as the art of a minority under the rule of empires, the literature of the State of Israel, which is a post-imperialist, majority literature of great richness and complexity, is reserved as the topic of a separate book.

Parts of this book were published in somewhat different form by the *British Journal of Sociology, Nations and Nationalism, Israel Affairs* and the London School of Economics as well as in *Imperialism and Biblical Prophecy 750–500 BCE*.

This book owes much to the two universities to which I have had the good fortune of being affiliated in recent years. McGill University provided a liberal and peaceful oasis where I had much encouragement from colleagues and students. I am also very grateful to my colleagues at the LSE, especially Professor Eileen Barker, for giving me the conditions in which this book came to fruition.

I thank McGill University and the Institute of Jewish Studies, London, for grants which helped the writing of this book in its final stages.

I am thankful, too, to the Department of Hebrew and Jewish Studies, University College, London, where I was privileged to be visiting professor during a sabbatical leave in 1992–3, and where I gave a series of lectures through which this book took its final shape.

A number of colleagues have read and responded to this book, or parts of it, in manuscript. In particular, I thank Professor John Hall of McGill University and Professor Martin Goodman of Oxford University for their penetrating criticisms.

I am also grateful to Dr Sarah Potter of Southampton University, and Professor Fergus Millar of Oxford University, for helpful advice on mission in the Roman empire and after.

I thank my editors, Mr Tim Farmiloe and Ms Aruna Vasudevan at Macmillan, and Ms Anne Rafique, for their invaluable help.

My wife, Mimi, has as always been a marvellous support throughout the writing of this book, which has been greatly enlivened by the birth of our three splendid children, Gabriella, Shulamit and Jessica, thus making this book itself the work of a minority.

In Italy for thirty years under the Borgias they had warfare, terror, murder and bloodshed, but they produced Michelangelo, Leonardo da Vinci and the Renaissance. In Switzerland, they had brotherly love; they had five hundred years of democracy and peace — and what did they produce? The cuckoo clock.

Graham Greene, *The Third Man*

Introduction: Toward a Sociological *Gestalt*

Hebrew has unique sociological interest as the oldest, in some ways most successful, minority literature. It is a Grand Canyon of civilization, with visible strata of most of the major cultures created over the past 3,000 years. While Hebrew is central specifically in the social history of the Jews, it also offers a panoramic view into the general nature of minority literatures, their relationship with the majority culture, and into the significance of literary creativity in ethnic survival.

On 14 May 1948, when the State of Israel came into being, Hebrew overnight stopped being the literature of a minority under non-Jewish rule. How did it survive with such remarkable tenacity and, at times, revolutionary creativity? One does not have to be a disciple of Marx to see that, to a very large extent, dominant powers and their cultures can crush minority cultures, whether through coercion, social pressure, or the force of their values and aesthetics, or through a mixture of these. In 'The German Ideology' (1845–6), Marx wrote: 'The ideas of the ruling class are in every epoch the ruling ideas: i.e. the class which is the ruling *material* force of society, is at the same time its ruling *intellectual* force' (1972, p. 172). Among the Jews traditionally, alone among minorities in the long term, the dominant external intellectual forces never overwhelmed their religious-national identity, but were absorbed into Judaism, usually via Hebrew writings.

Almost every individual feature of Hebrew literature has some parallel in other literatures. Yet the peculiar confluence of social and historical circumstances and literary qualities of Hebrew is unique. Its historical 'character' is distinct: as a sacred literature, the archetypal countercultural literature of protest (both against non-Jewish powers and beliefs and also against Jewish rule and practices), the first literature to be banned and its authors and teachers imprisoned or put to death, the only literature of the ancient world to survive as part of a living modern culture. As the literature of a minority, Hebrew has had disproportionate influence on the culture of the majority, to the point of being in a sense a majority culture *manqué* via Christianity and Islam.

1

Hebrew is unusual, too, in producing in its earliest phase a body of literature – only a small part of which has survived as the Bible – universally regarded as aesthetically and morally superior to the majority culture – that of the Mesopotamian empires – in which it was written. (In each succeeding phase of its development, in contrast, Hebrew literature is at best equal and for the most part inferior artistically to the finest literature in the dominant culture – this is especially true of Hebrew in Tsarist Russia.) At the same time, Hebrew has immersed itself chameleon-like as no other literature has in every major culture in which the Jews lived. Yet it has paradoxically remained unified, with clear influences in each period from preceding strata. The single binding force in all Hebrew creativity is the Hebrew Bible (Sáenz-Badillos, 1993).[1]

The growth of Hebrew literature in its various social settings is a fruitful area for sociological study. Yet only the Bible has received close attention by sociologists (Mayes, 1989), with Weber's *Ancient Judaism* the *locus classicus* of sociological research. This failure may be attributed largely to the comparatively recent development of sociology of literature and perhaps also to the fact that post-biblical Hebrew until the 19th century is rarely as interesting as the Bible. But it can also be traced in part to the tradition of Christian prejudice denying legitimacy to post-biblical Hebrew and Judaism. This prejudice has disappeared but its consequences are still felt. There has so far been no sociological study of Hebrew as part of a continuously evolving social organism. Neither has there been any serious attempt to discern patterns in the social development of Hebrew, particularly its relationship to the empires in which the majority of Jews lived from the time of the Bible until 1948.[2] This book aims, among other things, to make up for the neglect of Hebrew in the sociology of literature.

HEBREW AND JEWISH SURVIVAL

Throughout much of the history of the Jews, Jewish literature was written in languages other than Hebrew. Very little of this has survived from before the modern period. None was preserved with the reverence and loving care given to Hebrew. From the late biblical period, Hebrew was not part of the daily speech of the majority of Jews, even in Palestine. Already by the age of Augustus, prior to the exiles caused by the Roman–Jewish wars, most Jews lived outside Palestine. They used Hellenistic Greek and Aramaic far more than Hebrew as these were international languages vital in trade (Lieberman, 1950; Hengel, 1981). Aramaic kept its dominance for the next thousand years, until well after the Islamic conquest, when Arabic replaced it as the main language used by the Jews. In Europe by the Middle Ages, Yiddish became their *lingua franca* and remained so until the Holocaust. Since the late 19th century, Jews have contributed substantially to virtually every major European literature. Non-Hebrew Jewish literatures go back over two thousand years. Yet none of these has the moral passion and grandeur of Hebrew. None – not even Yiddish – has been as vital to Jewish identity and survival nor has had so long a history as Hebrew literature. Hebrew is the only common language uniting the socially disparate groups of Ashkenazic (European) and Sephardic (Oriental) Jews; and this too was an important factor in its survival. For these reasons, this book is concerned exclusively with Hebrew creativity, though without diminishing the importance of other languages.

Even during its periods of relative neglect – and these were many – Hebrew was used in prayer and study and regularly experimented with and kept alive artistically. Its survival as part of Judaism was never in doubt. Hebrew throughout history has been the single most authentic artistic expression of the Jewish spirit and of the Jewish will to live. If not for Hebrew, it is possible that the Jews and Judaism might not have survived and that the State of Israel might never have come into being.

FOUR PEAKS OF HEBREW LITERATURE: A *GESTALT*

From the time of the invention of the alphabet (Hebrew: *alephbet*) at the start of the first millennium BCE until 1948, Hebrew literature evolved continually under a string of powerful, doomed empires, each with a leading culture. These include: Mesopotamia in the biblical age, Rome in the talmudic era, Islamic Spain in the Middle Ages, and Tsarist Russia in modern times. Hebrew was also written elsewhere, in most countries in which the Jews were scattered. Yet the bulk of *artistic* achievement in Hebrew – much of the Bible and Talmud, medieval Hebrew poetry at its best and the successful transformation of Hebrew into a modern language and literature – was written in or derives from these empires. Hebrew literature has grown in fits and starts, with more periods of pale imitation, decline and stagnation than of brilliant achievement. Still, an unusual quantity of the best and most revolutionary Hebrew literature, with poetry its forte, was compressed into four periods totalling about five hundred years:

1. *750–500 BCE.* From the fall of the kingdom of Israel until the restoration of the state of Judah, a large part of the Bible – notably the prophetic works – was either written or edited. During this time, the Mesopotamian empires which ruled and annihilated Israel and Judah reached the height of their power. Then they fell apart and vanished. Although the Judean monarchy ended when the Temple in Jerusalem was burned down in 586 BCE and many Judeans were exiled by the Babylonians, Hebrew survived both in the diaspora and in Judah after the Judeans were allowed by Persia to return.

2. *66–200 CE.* In the first half of this period, the Jews were crushed in three wars against Rome (66–73, 115–17, 132–5 CE). These were the ultimate, most serious military challenges to Rome within the empire. They were also the last instances of organized Jewish military resistance prior to 1903, in Tsarist Russia. The destruction of the Second Temple in Jerusalem in 70 CE was a fatal blow to the priesthood and to centralized worship in Jerusalem. Synagogues and rabbis took their place, with Roman tolerance, and sermons as well as exegetical discussion – Midrash – became for many generations the main form of creativity in Hebrew (Bialik and Ravnitsky, 1992). The legal rulings and sayings of the rabbis, and anecdotes by and about them, were faithfully preserved until they were written down at a later date.[3] These comprise much of the Mishna (*c*.200 CE, the basis of talmudic discussions) and the halakhic[*] midrashim (chief of which are the *Mekhilta*, *Sifra* and *Sifre*). All these contain artistry of exceptional originality, in form and content.

3. *1031–1140.* Post-talmudic Hebrew until 1948 was primarily created in the Jewish diaspora, particularly in Mesopotamia, North Africa and Europe. While Hebrew poetry was written in practically every part of the diaspora (Carmi, 1981), the most important body of this poetry appeared during the 'golden age' of Hebrew poetry in Muslim Spain in the 11th and 12th centuries. This period coincided with the fall of the Umayyad empire and the almost constant civil

---

[*] Pertaining to the Halakhah (Jewish law).

wars which followed among the Muslim splinter kingdoms into which the empire degenerated. Meanwhile, the Christian armies in Northern Spain moved sporadically southwards. Two invasions of North African Berber tribes around 1090 and 1140 put an end to the Andalusian Jewish community and exiled Hebrew poetry. The main group of Hebrew poets between the time of Second Isaiah (late 6th century BCE) and Chaim Nachman Bialik (1873–1934), the leading modern Hebrew poet, lived during this period: Samuel Hanagid, Solomon ibn Gabirol, Moses ibn Ezra and Judah Halevi. Influenced decisively by Arabic poetry, these poets brought in many innovations in subject matter and versification. Though much of their poetry was liturgical they also created the first body of secular poetry in Hebrew.

4. *1881–1917.* After the Spanish period, Hebrew literature in the diaspora underwent relatively little significant artistic development until the 19th century, in Tsarist Russia. This does not mean that it is necessarily poor. Hebrew written in 16th century Ottoman Palestine or 18th century Italy (notably works of Moses Hayyim Luzzatto), for example, includes works of enduring beauty and charm. It is, nevertheless, largely imitative of the 'golden age' in medieval Spain. Only after the outbreak of pogroms in Russia until the 1917 revolution did Hebrew grow to become a significant, if still minor, force in modern literature. The Hebrew revival was based largely in Odessa and led by Mendele Mocher Sefarim (pen name of S. J. Abramowitz, 1835?–1917) in prose fiction and by Bialik in poetry (Aberbach, 1988, 1993). These writers were inspired to varying degrees by the rise of Jewish nationalism. They comprised a movement which, by using the full richness of the Hebrew literary tradition (which at the time it was still possible for one person to master in a lifetime), transformed Hebrew into a modern literature with Western European artistic standards. This revolution in Hebrew language and literature became the cultural basis of the new Palestinian Jewish community and, after 1948, of the State of Israel.

Much important Hebrew literature was lost and much was written between these four exceptionally innovative periods: for example, works included in the Apocrypha, the Pseudepigrapha and the Dead Sea Scrolls; in *hekhalot** poetry and in *piyyutim*** in Palestine under

*'[Heavenly] Halls': mystical poetry (*c.*3rd–7th centuries CE).
**Hebrew: sing. *piyyut*, from Greek *poiētēs*, 'to make': synagogue poetry which began in Byzantine Palestine and continued for many centuries.

Byzantine rule; in Hebrew poetry of medieval France and Germany as well as Christian Spain; in Italy from the Middle Ages until the 19th century; in 16th century Ottoman Palestine; in the Haskalah (Hebrew: Enlightenment) literature from the mid-18th century until 1881; in Palestine of the British mandate; and in the United States mainly prior to 1948. In addition, there is a large body of post-Mishnaic halakhic and exegetical writings in Hebrew some of which, in Rashi or Maimonides for example, has artistic merit.

HEBREW AESTHETICS AND SOCIAL CRISIS

Here it may be asked: what does artistic merit mean? What are the grounds for arguing that the prophetic and *tannaic** periods, the 'golden age' of Hebrew poetry in medieval Spain, and the Hebrew written in the final years of the Tsarist empire are on a higher aesthetic level than most of the extant Hebrew written at other times prior to 1948? The issue is, to some extent, subjective and should, ideally, be dealt with through close comparative readings of Hebrew texts, which is beyond the scope of this work. Yet, the question of aesthetic value is central to the argument here: that certain social and political circumstances appear to be more con-ducive to high artistic achievement than others.

Critical opinion tends to divide Hebrew literature into four main periods: biblical, talmudic, medieval and modern (Sáenz-Badillos, 1993). Within these periods, few scholars would argue against the claim that the prophetic and *tannaic* eras, the 'golden age' of medieval Hebrew poetry and the 1881–1917 period in Tsarist Russia are artistic peaks. However, it should be pointed out that Hebrew scholar-ship is mostly linguistic, theological and historical in character. Aes-thetic value is not generally among the foremost concerns of Hebrew scholars. In fact, the uniformed reader of certain studies on the Dead Sea Scrolls, the Genizah, and other bodies of Hebrew whose impor-tance is largely historical or theological, might mistakenly conclude that these are of artistic value equal to that of the prophets. Hebrew scholars tend to specialize in particular areas, periods and approaches. There is, so far, no single literary-critical work covering the development of Hebrew as art from the Bible to the present.

*From Hebrew 'Tanna' = teacher. A tanna is a rabbi of the Mishna, i.e. first two centuries CE.

It might be argued that survival itself reflects critical opinion and aesthetic judgement. Much pre-modern Hebrew survived as part of a sacred body of literature which only the Jews preserved in the original. Would they (and, for that matter, orthodox Christians and Muslims, who also regard the prophets as sacred) have believed this literature to be sacred and true had it not been beautiful? Yet, the Keatsian principle that 'Beauty is truth, truth beauty' is hardly convincing to the secular modern reader, who might be hard-pressed to comprehend the interest and value of much modern, let alone ancient, literary art.

A more acceptable criterion is originality. The events and personalities in each of the four periods outlined above, especially the prophets, set a permanent mould in the artistic character of Hebrew literature, more than in other periods of its creative growth. It is impossible to understate the originality of the prophets. They made an aesthetic revolution not just in Hebrew but also, ultimately, in Western and much Eastern civilization. In some ways, Weber (1961) argues, they prepared the ground for the modern world. Their emphasis on internal, abstract reality in metaphors and religious concepts, their intense social conscience, violent opposition to magic and superstition, and their criticism of the status quo, have no parallel in other surviving ancient near eastern texts. This language is familiar, so much so that we forget how shockingly new it must have been, much as we forget how radical were the Metaphysical poets, the Romantics and the Modernists in their day. 'I will betroth you to me in faith' (Hosea 2:21), 'you've made justice poison' (Amos 6:12), 'fountains of salvation' (Isaiah 12:3), 'to go humbly with your God' (Micah 6:8), 'circumcision of the heart' (Jeremiah 3:4), 'like a fire shut in my bones' (ibid. 20:9), 'a God in hiding' (Isaiah 45:15), 'prisoners of hope' (Zechariah 9:12). The language of the prophets points to a quality of mind substantially different from that which prevailed in the ancient world. The mind capable of such abstractions will not be content with material reality alone. The imagination must work harder, enriching itself in the struggle.

Consequently, nothing in Hebrew before or for 2,500 years after the prophets remotely approaches their particular form of artistic achievement: it is *sui generis*. In fact, the literature of the prophets evidently ended for the most part with the return of the Judean exiles and the building of the Second Temple in Jerusalem in the late 6th century BCE. Only with the rise of modern Jewish nationalism was prophetic poetry revived, notably in the writings of Bialik and U.Z. Greenberg.

Apart from prophetic poetry, what else is new in Hebrew? Midrash is the main body of Hebrew art after the prophets. It is dependent on biblical authority but contains much striking originality in language and ideas. Judging from the available evidence, the aggadic* and midrashic rabbinic style came to full fruition in oral form, if not in writing, in the generations following the destruction of the Second Temple in 70 CE. Sociologically and psychologically this development had its chief origins in the reconstitution of Judaism around the synagogue. This meant sermons by rabbis and imaginative development of aggadic as well as halakhic thought. During the *tannaic* period, Midrash 'reached a high point never since surpassed' (Epstein, 1959, p. 116). Though midrash continued for at least a millennium after the *tannaic* period, its form and content did not change substantially (de Lange, 1987, p. 157). The same appears to be true of halakhah after 200 CE, according to Daube (1949): 'there was a distinct lack of vitality and originality, the most prominent tendency now being ever greater specialization' (p. 334). The decline of Hebrew creativity under Roman rule, as under medieval Islam, coincided with a decline in the general culture (cf. MacMullen, 1988, pp. 4–5).

Enough is known about the social and political origins of prophetic poetry and the Midrash of the *tannaic* era to link the aesthetic leap in each period to specific historical crises. In addition it is possible that a third new Hebrew genre – *piyyut* (Petuchowski, 1978) – which developed also in the Land of Israel, in the 3rd– 7th centuries CE, was stimulated by international crisis and violent social change: the fall of the Roman empire in the 5th century CE and the rise of Islam in the 7th century CE, which brought Palestine under Islamic rule. The *Gestalt* presented here strongly argues for such a link. Unfortunately, much of the period from the 3rd to the 7th century CE is a historical blank. Even the approximate dates of the greatest *paytanim* of the period – Kallir, Yose ben Yose, Yannai – are uncertain (Carmi, 1981). Even so, as in the case of secular Hebrew poetry, religious Hebrew poetry reached its artistic high point during the Spanish Muslim period: 'later *paytanim* failed to create major works' (Fleischer, 1971, 13:598).

---

* Aggadah refers to everything in the Talmud which is not halakhah, e.g. legend, anecdote and historical material.

As Midrash did not undergo substantial change after the 2nd century, so also, though to a lesser extent, Hebrew poetry (especially secular poetry) did not change greatly after the 'golden age' (Carmi, 1981, p. 32ff.).[4] Medieval and modern Hebrew writers, though revolutionary in the growth of Hebrew literature, have a smaller claim than the prophets and the *tannaim* to originality on a world scale. They tend to introduce genres, themes and techniques from other literatures. Judah Halevi, for example, is a major figure in medieval Hebrew but is not equal to Dante or Chaucer in world literature.

In Tsarist Russia in the 1881–1917 period, similarly, Mendele and Bialik break little new ground in world literature. They are outstandingly original in the renaissance of Hebrew literature. During this period, in fact, there was 'a galaxy of talented writers who raised modern Hebrew literature from mere publicistic and didactic writing to the realm of art' (Patterson, 1985a, p. 4). Outstanding modern Hebrew literature was written in empires other than Tsarist Russia – notably Austro-Hungary and Turkish Palestine prior to 1917 and Palestine under the British mandate until 1948. Yet, the main cultural impetus for this literature came from the Tsarist empire and was transplanted in Palestine during the Second Aliyah (1904–14). The combination of the social and political conditions and revolutionary artistry in Tsarist Russia was not repeated elsewhere. The most important Hebrew writers born into the Austro-Hungarian empire – the Nobel laureate, S. J. Agnon and U.Z. Greenberg – produced much of their main work in mandatory Palestine and in the early days of the State of Israel.[5] Their work owes little either to Austro-Hungary or to British culture. The most profound and lasting literary influences on their work came from Russian Hebrew writers: above all, Mendele, whose ironic, mock-rabbinic prose fiction was the chief stylistic influence on Agnon; and Bialik, whose neo-prophetic verse was decisive in Greenberg's artistic evolution. The main poetic innovator in Hebrew under British rule in Palestine, Abraham Shlonsky, was born in Tsarist Russia and was influenced primarily by Russian Hebrew poets and by Russian modernists such as Blok, Esenin and Mayakovsky. The seminal achievement in reviving spoken Hebrew and creating an original Hebrew literature of internationally recognized importance, and an artistic standard against which many Israeli writers continue to measure their own literary achievements, was that of the Russian Jews in the Tsarist empire, mainly during the period 1881–1917.

Influence, then, may be seen as a gauge of aesthetic significance. The prophets were decisive in the growth of world literature and, indeed, of civilization. Many of the salient qualities of prophetic poetry – its imagination, insight and its power to inspire; its depth of feeling, linguistic daring and ingenuity; its bold metaphor and rhythm, compression and musicality – form the artistic basis for much pre-modern and modern literature. Midrash is less well-known but has been, nevertheless, a significant force, particularly through the development of Christian homiletics, as recent scholars (e.g. in Hartman and Budick, 1986) have come increasingly to recognize. However, post-talmudic Hebrew has had relatively little influence outside the Jewish world up to 1948.

One last comment on literary quality: Hebrew literature at its most free and natural, when it most successfully marries form to content and creates a world of the imagination which the reader can most fully 'live in', is mainly literature created in the Land of Israel.

The criteria for including the four periods listed in the *Gestalt* sketched above may be summed up as follows: they are highly original in the context of the growth of Hebrew literature; they represent an artistic leap forward determining the character of later Hebrew literature; and they are linkable in content and chronology to specific social and political crises in the life of empires. Much Hebrew literature produced between these periods might be traced to parallel circumstances but rarely in such a pronounced, far-reaching way. With some exceptions, they are secondary as *art*.

HEBREW, EMPIRE AND CRISIS

Why did Hebrew literature flourish artistically when it did and as it did? Can a sociological pattern be detected in which Hebrew literature in its most original and influential phases is stimulated by a particular set of social and political circumstances? What is its connection with empires and their vicissitudes? In which ways was it influenced by the cultures of these empires? Why is the picture of empires and their cultures in Hebrew literature so sketchy and misleading? Why did Hebrew literature succeed in some periods more than in others? What is the relationship between Hebrew literature and Judaism and Jewish survival? Is there generally a link between aesthetics and social and political change? These are some of the questions to be explored in this book.

How might the argument here – that the main peaks of Hebrew literature prior to 1948 were closely linked to upheavals in the empires in which they were created as well as to the culture of these empires – be justified? A number of outstanding sociological elements are common to each bout of creativity. These, taken together, are without parallel in other periods in the development of Hebrew literature. They include: social and political instability bringing about a decline in imperial power or the annihilation of empires; considerable military activity and economic expansion producing major changes in the international balance of power and substantially affecting the course of civilization; outbursts of violence against Jews and the exile or migration of large numbers of Jews (including many Hebrew writers); a consequent distortion or arrestation of a natural process of Jewish assimilation into a brilliant dominant culture; the decline or disappearance of longstanding Jewish institutional authority. To the powerless, Hebrew was a source of power; to the divided, it gave unity; to the victims of injustice and oppression, it gave hope. It was a means of competitive imitation *vis-à-vis* the dominant culture. It was a retreat into ethnic nationalism. It asserted cultural superiority and resistance. It was an act of spiritual revolt and revival. The pattern, though rough, is consistent.

The social and political conditions of Hebrew creativity are treated here as inseparable from the ethnic survival of the Jews. The role of Hebrew in Jewish survival helps to explain the general relationship between dominant cultures and minorities, between crisis, nationalism and creativity. Hebrew is the only minority culture that can be studied in its development over a period of nearly 3,000 years. It illumines other striking periods of creativity associated with crisis: for example, the classical age of Greek tragedy, the age of Confucianism, the High Renaissance, the ages of romanticism and of modernism. The connection between crisis and creativity has been noted by sociologists of literature. Goldmann (1964), for example, has observed: 'On the social as well as the individual plane, it is the sick organ which creates awareness, and it is in moments of crisis that men are most aware of the enigma of their presence in the world' (p. 49). This insight has not previously been applied to Hebrew literature in the various phases of its growth.

The role of Hebrew as the authentic voice of Jewish self-preservation and renewal in moments of crisis recalls the pre-war joke about the elegant Parisian woman about to give birth while trying to hide her east European Jewish origins. She does not realize that her doctor is also Jewish and knows her secret. As long as she groans in French, the doctor advises his assistant to wait. Finally, she shrieks, '*Ribbono shel olam!*'* 'Maintenant,' the doctor says, 'le temps est arrivé.'

IMPERIALISM AND HEBREW

Even a skeletal account of the main creative periods of Hebrew literature draws the reader to a striking relationship between the vicissitudes of pre-industrial empires and Hebrew creativity.[6] Hebrew developed almost entirely within the orbit of empires. An understanding of imperialism is therefore vital in understanding why and how Hebrew literature grew as it did. Scholarly interpretations of imperialism began in the late 19th century, with modern empires their main subjects. However, most scholars agree that these interpretations apply to the ancient and medieval empires as well, inasmuch as the human forces underlying imperialism have not changed greatly and its means and ends remain fundamentally the same (cf. Garnsey and Whittaker, 1978; Aberbach, 1993a). Historical and theoretical evidence suggests that imperialism results from a number of factors, some of which have had an incalculable influence on the development of Hebrew literature. These include: nationalism, geographic and economic pressure; the drive for power and prestige; greed, cruelty and raw energy; the struggle for security; and, surprisingly, even humanitarianism and a desire to enlighten.

Each of the empires in which Hebrew flourished had a different set of motives, aims and circumstances. Their Jewish communities were highly variegated as was the Hebrew literature in each empire. This literature, especially that of 1881–1917, represents a radical break with the past while at the same time continuing the Hebrew literary tradition.

HEBREW LITERATURE AND THE DECLINE OF EMPIRES

Napoleon once said that empires die of indigestion. Each outstanding period of pre-1948 Hebrew literature is characterized by strik-

---

* Hebrew and Yiddish: 'Master of the Universe'.

ing economic expansion in the dominant empire, which paradoxically – through the creation or exacerbation of unrest, corruption, disunity and international conflict – appears to accompany or even contribute to the empire's decline and ultimate collapse. The prophets, for example, witnessed the total disappearance of the Assyrian and Babylonian empires. The *tannaim* were part of a huge Roman empire struggling, unsuccessfully in the end, to maintain control, cohesion and unity. They saw the beginning of a process – the salient features of which were the rise of Christianity in the 1st century CE and the invasion of barbarian tribes from central Europe in the 2nd century CE – which led to the destruction of the empire by the 6th century CE. The 'golden age' of Hebrew poetry in the 11th and 12th centuries CE was a time of violent turbulence and decline for the Islamic empire in Western Europe and North Africa. It was a time of civil war and increasing Islamic fanaticism, which the Hebrew poets experienced personally. These upheavals enter their poems which, on one level, may be seen as artistic records of the state of the Spanish Jewish community in a collapsing Muslim empire. Imperial weakness was also a cause of the Hebrew revival of 1881–1917. After the Crimean war, the political and economic difficulties faced by Tsarist Russia were crucial factors in the Jewish national-cultural revival.

CHANGES IN THE BALANCE OF POWER

Imperial crisis heralded a shift of power crucial in the history of civilization – from the Near East to Europe in the biblical age, from pagan Rome to Christianity in the talmudic epoch, from Islam to Christianity in medieval Europe, from Tsarist autocracy to revolutionary socialism in modern Russia. In each period, furthermore, the Jews were caught between two major forces in conflict: between Egypt and Mesopotamia in the biblical era; between Rome and Parthia in the time of the Talmud; between Islam and Christianity in medieval Spain; and between Western liberal enlightenment and violent Slavophile nationalism in the Romanov empire.

HEBREW AND THE FAILURE OF JEWISH ASSIMILATION

The Jews immediately prior to the four periods of Hebrew literature outlined above were in a gradual process of assimilation within the empires. The weakening of each empire arrested or distorted this development, first through non-Jewish revulsion, discrimination and violence against the Jews, then through the resultant Jewish separatism and retreat into a distinct religious-cultural-national identity at the core of which is Hebrew and the Hebrew Bible.

Both biblical and extra-biblical evidence indicates that at the start of the prophetic period, the Israelites were thoroughly assimilated into near eastern pagan culture. When defeated by the Assyrians in 721 BCE, they were exiled together with their gods. The Nimrud Prism of Sargon II reports that on capturing Samaria, Israel's capital, Sargon carried away 'the gods in whom they trusted' (Thomas, 1958, p. 60). Consequently, Israel's national identity faded in exile, and Hebrew as well as monotheism survived only in Judah. By the end of the prophetic era two centuries later, the Jews were broken by imperial crisis, defeat and exile. They responded by totally breaking with near eastern religion through the acceptance of an exclusive abstract monotheism with Hebrew its sacred language.

The dynamics of the biblical world seem to have set the pattern for later Jewish relationships with empires: assimilation and the neglect of Hebrew in normal conditions, and separatism, Jewish nationalism and Hebrew creativity in crisis. Prior to the Roman–Jewish war of 66–73 CE, the Jews again – especially the upper classes – were increasingly assimilated into Graeco-Roman culture. Greek and Aramaic took the place of Hebrew among the majority of Jews. But then came defeat, humiliation and exile coupled with imperial crisis which derailed many Jews from the track of assimilation. By the start of the 3rd century, rabbinic Judaism and Hebrew in study, homiletics and prayer (and, to a lesser extent, spoken Hebrew) were firmly established as a minority culture within the empire. External influences were at least nominally shunned by many rabbis.

In a similar way, the Spanish Jews at the start of the 'golden age' of Hebrew poetry in the 10th century were so assimilated into Arabic culture that their main language was Arabic. Some Jews emulated courtly ideals of behaviour and aesthetics in the hope of achieving full acceptance in Islamic society. For a short period this hope was realized to an extent unique in Arab–Jewish history. Then came the collapse of the Umayyad empire, civil war, the spread of Islamic fundamentalism, anti-Semitic violence and exile – and again profound disillusionment with the dominant culture. By the end of the 'golden age' Hebrew was used to push Jewish nationalism. The main Hebrew poet of the age, Judah Halevi, left Andalusia for Palestine in 1140.

Finally, the Russian Jews during the comparatively liberal rule of Alexander II (1855–81) were becoming more 'russified' as time passed. They sent their children to Russian schools and universities in relatively large numbers and played an increasing role in the economic and cultural life of the empire. The pogroms of 1881–4 undermined the process of russification. Imperial weakness, expressed in anti-Semitic policies, turned the Russian Jews in on themselves. As the Tsarist empire collapsed, the Jews became sharply aware of their distinctiveness, of their national identity – and their Hebrew culture.

DEMOGRAPHIC CHANGE: JEWISH MIGRATION AND HEBREW LITERATURE

In each crisis, Hebrew culture grew simultaneously with a large movement of Jewish population – from Palestine to Mesopotamia and Egypt in the biblical age; from Palestine to virtually every part of the Roman empire in talmudic times; from Spain to North Africa, Palestine and various European countries in the Middle Ages; and from the Russian Pale of Settlement to North America, Palestine and elsewhere after 1881. The demographic shift was, in part, a natural process extending over many centuries. However, this movement of population was greatly increased by violence against Jews which drove them to exile: the Israelites by Assyria in the late 8th century BCE; the Judeans by Babylonia in the early 6th century BCE and, again, during and after the wars with Rome in the 1st and 2nd centuries CE; the Spanish Jews after the Berber invasions in the 11th and 12th centuries; and the Russian Jews during and after the pogroms of 1881–4 and 1903–6. Exile and mourning are among the chief causes and motifs of Hebrew literature provoked by these upheavals.

HEBREW AND EGALITARIANISM

Hebrew authors, whether of oral or written literature, are distinguished as a class through the ages by the insignificance of class differences among them. Their 'calling' or learning gained them a special status. Hebrew, then, uniquely among pre-modern literatures, was not the province of the upper classes. It was created by shepherds as well as priests, blacksmiths as well as princes. For example, the prophet Amos, a shepherd, is the equal of Jeremiah the priest. Among the rabbis of the *tannaic* age, social background and class had relatively little significance:

> It is remarkable, particularly in the status-conscious society of the second century Roman Empire, that the Jewish intelligentsia of this period [included] manual labourers, but there is no doubt that this was so.
>
> (Goodman, 1983, p. 93)

Similarly, the medieval Hebrew writers were spiritual and artistic leaders by virtue not of aristocratic birth but of merit. The child of the humblest Jew could in theory gain a Hebrew education and produce Hebrew religious poetry accepted as sacred and used in the liturgy. Hebrew writers in Tsarist Russia, unlike many of their Russian contemporaries (e.g. Turgenev, Dostoevsky, Tolstoy), came mostly from among the poor and the working class. Bialik, for example, was the son of a tavern keeper. These writers, though they mostly broke with traditional Judaism, were an elite as Hebrew writers.

In each period, then, Hebrew literature cut across class differences, speaking for a fundamental unity of the Jewish people based upon religious and/or national beliefs and identity rather than class, wealth and status. The need for this egalitarianism appears to have been especially pronounced in crisis, when class differences among the Jews could be dangerous. The unity promoted by a common set of beliefs and practices, a collective history, language and literature, enhanced the chances of Jewish survival.

EXILE OF HEBREW WRITERS

A disproportionate number of important Hebrew writers were exiled or uprooted from their place of origin. For example, among the major prophets at least two – Jeremiah and Ezekiel – are known to have been exiled as a direct result of imperial conquest. The Mishna was written down and edited in Galilee by rabbis who were for the most part either exiles or sons of exiles from Judaea after the

Bar-Kokhba revolt of 132–5 CE. After the revolt and until the 4th century CE, the Romans banned Jewish residence in Jerusalem and much of Judaea in an attempt to crush surviving vestiges of militant Jewish nationalism. Likewise, all the most important Hebrew poets of the 'golden age' in medieval Spain were exiles in one way or another. Of the major Russian-born Hebrew writers of the 1881–1917 period, almost all left Russia never to return.

DECLINE OF JEWISH RELIGIOUS AUTHORITY

The growth of Hebrew in each period was accompanied by a drastic fall or disappearance of the defining authority in Jewish life. The Davidic monarchy of Judah, greatly weakened by Assyria in the 8th century BCE, did not survive the Babylonian exile in the 6th century BCE. The fall of the monarchy enhanced the authority of the prophets and their poetry and created circumstances in which the concept of the Bible became both artistically possible and spiritually vital. Similarly, the eradication by the Romans of the Temple priesthood in 70 CE left a vacuum filled by rabbinic Judaism and its major Hebrew accomplishments, in the Talmud and Midrash. In the Middle Ages, likewise, the decline of Babylonian Jewry and its rabbinate and the disappearance in 1038 of the Gaonate – the main institution of rabbinic authority since the birth of Islam – ran parallel and was in some ways connected with the eclipse of the eastern Abbasid empire by the western Umayyad empire. Finally, the decline of the Romanov empire in 1881–1917 and, to a lesser extent, in the quarter-century prior to 1881 was accompanied by a fall in the authority of the east European rabbinate and the wholesale defection of Jews from traditional Judaism.

A BRILLIANT DOMINANT CULTURE

At the same time as these crises and virtually as part of them, each empire created a culture which in many ways was the most advanced in history up to that time and which had an immense, if largely unacknowledged, impact upon Hebrew. In each empire with the exception of the Mesopotamian ones in which most of the Bible was created, Hebrew literature was the outstanding surviving contribution to literary civilization after the dominant culture. When the indigenous non-Jewish culture was not highly developed – in medieval Germany or France, for example – Hebrew literature tended to imitate the Palestinian or Spanish schools and was of a lower artistic quality than the literature written within the leading empires. Hebrew stood apart from the civilizations of these empires while at the same time forming a part of them. It, too, was mostly an urban phenomenon, though each empire, including Tsarist Russia, was predominantly agrarian, and there were numerous ignorant Jews in rural areas. Yet, the liturgical uses of Hebrew meant that the language and literature were accessible to a far larger proportion of readers than, say, the Latin of Virgil was in the Roman empire, the poetry of Ibn Zaidun was in the medieval empire of Islam, or Dostoevsky's *Crime and Punishment* was in Tsarist Russia. In the talmudic period, as indicated earlier, the growth of Hebrew was linked with the rise of synagogue culture and also with the phenomenal development of Jewish education, the first educational system aimed not at an elite but at the masses. Jewish education has been an integral part of Jewish life until the present day. It has ensured in each generation a substantial number of Jews who could read Hebrew and some who could write it. As a result, though the Jews in each empire formed a tiny minority, the proportion of literate Jews was exceptionally high.

HEBREW AND THE DOMINANT CULTURE: IMITATION AND COMPETITION

In its most intensely creative periods under the rule of empires, Hebrew entered into a mostly one-sided relationship of ambivalent imitation of and competition with a powerful culture which was almost totally ignorant of it and whose treatment of the Jews varied from tolerance to suspicion and violent persecution. At the same time, the degree of imitation was always greater than could be freely admitted: the sacredness of the Hebrew language and literature put them above the 'corrupt' and 'ungodly' empires in which they were written and above their cultures. Hebrew literature often creates the odd illusion that the Jews lived in an ahistorical time warp, and that Hebrew culture was largely independent of foreign influence. One would hardly guess from Hebrew literature that for most of Jewish history Mesopotamian, Graeco-Roman, Islamic and Tsarist empires determined the lives of most Jews and unintentionally created conditions in which the Jews and Judaism could survive and, at times, flourish materially and culturally.

CULTURAL SUPERIORITY, POLITICAL WEAKNESS

The Hebrew literature produced under the rule of these empires was on its own little more than a minor tributary of the general culture. The inseparable link between the Jews and the Bible, however, created for them an ever-awkward identity as a minority with a superior, ever-evolving civilization, not easily assimilated into the dominant culture, but itself attractive to large numbers of potential adherents. The culture of empires is bloodied by war and conquest. The Jews, as a perpetual minority, had the paradoxical advantage of being unable to compete militarily and being forced, therefore, to base their religious culture not upon military heroism and power but upon a philosophy of life considerably more humane than that of empires. The emphasis in Hebrew on the worship of one abstract God as the true imperial conqueror, demanding truth, faith, love and justice, was antithetical to, even subversive of, the realities of imperial rule (Aberbach, 1993a). Few literatures are more fiercely, even militantly, opposed to the abuse of power and more committed to social and political change than Hebrew. This literature consistently elevates the life of the spirit and sees imperial government as weak, amoral and persecutory.

It should be added that some of the literature of the dominant cultures which influenced Hebrew directly or indirectly contains elements of dissidence, protest and anti-imperialism in reaction to crisis: for example, the ancient Mesopotamian *Epic of Gilgamesh*, with its dismissal of the value of power, conquest and glory in the face of death; the disillusionment with power in the writings of Horace, Juvenal and especially Tacitus, among others, in the talmudic era; the relatively individualistic Arabic poetry of the 'golden age' which, like its contemporary Hebrew poetry, was stimulated by the lack of a political structure when the Umayyad empire fell; and the Russian writers in Tsarist Russia whose works in some ways constituted a challenge to totalitarian rule and anticipated the revolution. Still, Hebrew by virtue of being a sacred minority literature was *ipso facto* a countercultural phenomenon even when it appeared to serve the status quo. The potential for subversion was always there, though it rarely flared up in an active nationalistic or revolutionary form.

HEBREW LITERATURE: CULTURAL RESISTANCE, SPIRITUAL REVOLT

Many centuries passed, however, before empires began to regard the Jews and Judaism as a threat. In the age of the Mesopotamian empires, the Jews were left alone if they paid their taxes and did not revolt. The decline and fall of these empires confirmed the prophetic belief in the 'imperial rule' of the one invisible God who could not be annihilated as were the pagan empires and their gods. The Assyrian and Babylonian literary heritage survived as part of a living culture only in the Bible, notably in the mono-theistic versions of Mesopotamian myths such as the stories of the creation or the flood. But no evidence has been found that Assyria or Babylonia was ever aware of the existence of mono-theism in its empire. It may be that Judaism and Hebrew religious culture were so unthreatening to these empires that they were totally ignored. The Jews outlasted six pagan empires – Assyria, Babylonia, Persia, Macedonia, the Ptolemies and Seleucids, as well as several hundred years of Roman rule – as an isolated monotheistic nation.

The ultimate pagan empire, the Graeco-Roman, however, rightly saw Judaism as a serious rival to the Hellenistic culture through which the empire tried to unify its fissiparous parts. Hebrew litera-ture was decisively affected in the years 66–200 CE, though, as indicated earlier, much of it was written down at a later date. The character of Judaism and of Hebrew literature was changed by the Roman–Jewish wars, and the exile and pauperization which fol-lowed, by the attempt to ban Judaism and the consequent martyr-doms, by the emergence of anti-Semitism among the Hellenistic Greeks, and by the rise of Christianity (Schürer, 1973–87). These forces turned Hebrew in on itself. The Bible above all had made the uncritical acceptance of imperial culture unpalatable to most Jews who, intoxicated by the beauty and awe of their religion, believed themselves to be married eternally to God and to the Torah. As a result, the Jews already in the Hellenistic period (2nd century BCE) had become the first people in history to be targeted because of their religion, the first to have their sacred literature banned and destroyed, and the first to die for their faith. Their history made full acculturation extremely difficult. The social and psychological prob-lem in having a superior answer to Rome is illustrated bitingly in the Babylonian Talmud in the fate of the rabbi who ousts the emperor in debate and is punished by being thrown to the lions (*Sanhedrin* 38a).

DEFEAT AND HEBREW LITERATURE

To the extent that the Jews refused or failed to become integrated into the empire, or the empire failed to assimilate them, Hebrew rose in importance. It helped to master defeat and to create a new basis of Jewish life under Rome. It also gave voice to Jewish nationalism and even to the muted hope of ultimate universal acceptance of Judaism.

After the failure of the Bar-Kokhba revolt against Rome in 132–5 CE and the Hadrianic persecution which followed, a condition of Jewish survival in the Roman empire was the abdication of missionary activity. This ban was an implicit admission of the Roman fear of Judaism and of its immense potential attraction to pagans. In this way, Judaism fell into the trap of being, on the one hand, a universal religion, progenitor of Christianity and Islam with Hebrew as its chief mode of expression, and, on the other hand, confined almost exclusively to Jews. The teachings of the Hebrew Bible were spread through Christianity and Islam. Yet, post-biblical Hebrew remained until the 20th century largely closed within the Jewish world. As we have seen, two of the main forms of Hebrew creativity from Roman times until the 19th century are Midrash and *piyyut*. Both are uniquely Jewish genres requiring almost photographic knowledge of Scripture and virtually incomprehensible except among Jews. The turn inward of Judaism and Hebrew literature was later enhanced by the fact that neither Christianity nor Islam could accept the Hebrew Bible on its own terms, as a creation of Jews and an expression of Judaism. Rather, the chief value of the Hebrew Bible was as a harbinger of the 'new' religions, the aesthetics and theology of whose sacred literature derived admittedly from Hebrew literature.

HEBREW AND CULTURAL ASSIMILATION

Yet, as in other periods of Hebrew creativity, the dominant culture filled Jewish life. Throughout the talmudic period Jews lived in close proximity to Greeks. Before 70 CE, the Jewish aristocracy had adopted Hellenism as a culture in many ways superior to Judaism. Hebrew literature was infiltrated by Greek vocabulary and concepts. The Roman defeat of the Jews inhibited their assimilation into the empire but could not eliminate it totally. The entire system of rabbinic discussion of Jewish law which predominates in the Talmud and Midrash was influenced by the symposia of the Greek philosophers. Indeed, the rabbis were classed as philosophers by the Roman authorities (Baron, 1952, II, p. 243). In addition, the immense work in the 2nd and 3rd centuries CE on the codification of Roman law left its mark on the Mishna. The style of the Mishna – clear, concise, well-organized – recalls Latin legal writings. However, its imaginative, at times even surreal, artistic qualities and its influence on Hebrew writers – Agnon, for example, treated the Mishna as a model of pure Hebrew prose – mark it out from all other legal codes. In the rabbis' absorption with minutiae and the apparent seriousness with which they discuss matters which appear as trivial, their literature can sometimes be seen more as parody than imitation of Greek symposia and Roman law (e.g. *Pesaḥim* 10b, *Bezah* 2a, and *Bava Batra* 23b).

The collapse of the Roman empire in the 5th century CE left a power vacuum which was filled with the rise of Islam. The creative heart of Hebrew culture came under Arabic influence. The biblical and talmudic periods had produced works of enduring fascination while apparently lacking strict artistic rules. Medieval Islam created a labyrinthine system of poetics which had a considerable influence upon Hebrew at a time (8th–13th centuries) when the majority of the world Jewish population lived under Muslim rule (Pagis, 1971). During the 'golden age' of Hebrew poetry in 11th and 12th century Spain, Hebrew poets adopted the rigid rules of Arabic metrics, versification and subject-matter. Hebrew writers, notably Judah Halevi, were aware that the result was often shallow, repetitive and artificial (Brann, 1991). They were handicapped by the fact that in the Arabic models, poetry was mainly ornament, whereas in Hebrew, poetry was the basis for a way of life and faith. Yet, their enthralment by Arabic culture led to an immense expansion of Hebrew poetic technique and theory and a genre of 'secular', as opposed to liturgical, poetry which had not previously existed and which anticipates the largely secular character of modern Hebrew poetry. The impact of Arabic poetics on Hebrew far outlasted the empire in which it came into being. Hebrew did not return to free verse until 1897 – significantly, the year of the First Zionist Congress – when Bialik wrote the poem *Im yesh et nafshekha la-da'at* (If you want to know).

The Tsarist empire in which Bialik emerged as the most original and influential Hebrew poet since Judah Halevi was, for the most part, a cultural backwater in comparison with western Europe. However, even in the oppressive reign of Nicholas I (1825–55), Russian writers, notably Pushkin, Gogol and Lermontov, had produced poetry and fiction of genius. The reforms of Alexander II (1855–81) gave Russian literature the impetus to become the most important in Western civilization. Hebrew was more profoundly influenced by Russian literature than it had been by any literary culture since the medieval Islamic period. Perhaps inevitably Hebrew literature under Romanov rule was mostly of secondary importance alongside the 19th-century masterpieces of Russian literature. Still, this literature is a unique sociological phenomenon inasmuch as it accompanied the revival of Hebrew as a modern spoken and written language and acted as cultural midwife for political Zionism. Though socioeconomic distress played a part, as in other modern nationalisms (Hroch, 1985), the crucial spur in the Jewish national awakening was cultural. In this regard, it resembles other cultural nationalisms, such as those of the Slovaks within the Habsburg empire, the Greeks within the Ottoman empire, and the Irish within the British empire (Hutchinson, 1987).

THE TSARIST EMPIRE, ZIONISM AND HEBREW LITERATURE

The Jews in Russia – about one million – had come under Russian rule with the partitions of Poland in the late 18th century: previously, they had not been allowed to live in the Russian empire. By the end of the 19th century their numbers reached five million, the largest, most dynamic, yet backward and impoverished Jewish population in the world. Most of them were confined by law to the Pale of Settlement on the western border of the empire. During most of the 19th century, they were almost totally ignorant of secular learning. Liberal and reactionary forces contended either in encouraging the Jews to gain an education and become 'russified' or in condemning the Jews as Christ-killers and parasites, unwanted in Russia. During the first part of the reign of Alexander II, it seemed that liberalism would bring the Jews emancipation and civil rights. Hebrew during this period fitted into the liberal strategy, aiming to enlighten the Jewish masses. As had been shown in Germany in the 18th and early 19th centuries, Hebrew could serve as a tool whereby uneducated Jews could obtain some education, especially in the sciences.

The assassination of Alexander II in 1881 set off a violent anti-Semitic reaction and put an end to liberal hopes. From then until the 1917 revolution, Hebrew under Tsarist rule developed almost entirely as part of the rise of Jewish nationalism. Hebrew literature was influenced by Russian literature virtually to the point of being a branch of it, but it also marks a decisive break with Russia, a declaration of independence, part of the struggle for an independent political state. In many ways, too, it breaks with the Hebrew literary tradition, for it is the first wholly secular Hebrew literature written and read mostly by Jews (including for the first time an increasing number of women) who did not practise traditional Judaism. The Russian Hebrew writers, led by Mendele in prose fiction and by Bialik in poetry, helped to redefine modern Jewish identity along social and political, as opposed to religious, lines.

CONCLUSION

Many of the most notable advances in Hebrew literature prior to 1948 coincided with, and are probably inseparable from, periods in which unusually severe imperial turbulence and upheaval was combined with cultural efflorescence. In each period, the creation of original Hebrew literature became an exceptionally pressing concern in Jewish life. It was characterized by a dynamic group of men comprising a literary movement which brought about an aesthetic revolution and, to varying degrees, a social and psychological revolution. A number of interrelated elements appear in each period which are not found together – certainly not in the same intensity, if at all – at any other time. Most importantly, perhaps, were two factors: (a) a profound and justified sense of threat to Jewish survival; and (b) a brilliant civilization into which the Jews (or many of them) tried with limited success to become integrated and with which they tried to compete, again with only limited success, except for the Hebrew Bible. Other important elements underlying Hebrew culture during these periods include: a large Jewish population (though not more than 5–10 per cent of the total) which had lived under imperial rule for several generations at least and had time to become acculturated within the dominant culture; a dramatic growth in imperial military activity as well as violence directed specifically at Jews, which was symptomatic of instability or impending breakdown, and which naturally arrested the process of Jewish acculturation; and a major shift in the global balance of power and in Jewish demography, involving economic upheaval, mass migration and the decline or disappearance of the main religious authority in Jewish life.

Hebrew writers were traumatized and disoriented by rapid violent change and social disintegration into preserving for all time in the only uniquely Jewish language prior to 1948 a way of life feared to be in mortal danger. They galvanized Hebrew literature with the transcendent aesthetic and ideological properties of its sacred origins. In these moments of crisis, when Jewish survival was at stake and the forces of conservatism and routine broke down, Hebrew found its greatest artistic freedom and originality.

Hebrew literature, then, can be treated as a gauge of sociological phenomena. In its retreat to Jewish nationalism in moments of persecution, Hebrew literature is the archetypal cultural vehicle for minority nationalism. There is a clear, consistent link between severe military and psychic wounds dealt to the Jews by the dominant imperial power and Jewish nationalism, with its Hebrew creativity. It should be stressed, however, that parallel phenomena are found not only among other minorities and their literatures (e.g. 19th-century Polish or Ukrainian) but also, at times, in the cultures of the ruling powers. And indeed, as we have seen, Hebrew creativity in its artistic peaks is symbiotically bound to the brilliant creativity of the dominant culture in crisis.

Throughout its history, Hebrew is characterized by ambivalence toward the empires in which it was written, by admiration and hostility, and it gives a generally distorted picture of imperial rule and culture. Influenced decisively by this culture, it engaged in spiritual protest and revolt against it. It created instead a more narrow but secure Jewish religious and national identity. More than any other language, Hebrew served the Jewish people as an aesthetic 'safe territory' from the terror and disillusionment of unstable imperial rule. 'If we must suffer,' Ellmann (1968) writes of Yeats, 'it is better to create the world in which we suffer' (p. xxiv).

This truth may underlie the function of culture generally in periods of crisis. For example, the birth of tragedy in the drama of Aeschylus, Sophocles and Euripedes (5th century BCE) came in an age dominated by major wars, first between Greece and Persia, then between Athens and Sparta in the Peloponnesian wars. In the 5th–3rd centuries BCE Confucianism, likewise, emerged amid constant civil war in China. In the High Renaissance (*c.* 1495–1527), the explosion of original art by Leonardo, Michelangelo and Raphael was accompanied by frequent wars as France and Spain struggled for hegemony over Italy. Many of the artistic achievements of the Romantic movement – the poetry of Goethe and Wordsworth, the music of Beethoven and Schubert – were created under the impact of the French revolution and the Napoleonic wars. In the early 20th century, too, the creative flowering of writers such as Yeats, Joyce, Eliot and Pound, among others, was inseparably bound up with the massive blow to the ideals of Western civilization – the 'old bitch gone in the teeth' as Pound called it – in the First World War.

Despite the fundamental optimism of Judaism, the most lasting memories of empires in Hebrew are the negative ones: the destruction of Israel by the Assyrians in 721 BCE, the annihilation of Judah and the burning down of the Temple in Jerusalem by the Babylonians in 586 BCE and by the Romans in 70 CE, the massacres and expulsions under Islam and Christianity in the Middle Ages, the Russian pogroms of the late 19th and early 20th centuries. These memories are an indelible part of Hebrew literature. Yet the empires all allowed – in some cases facilitated – the survival of the Jews, of Judaism and of the Hebrew language. They stimulated a literary high culture which Hebrew literature emulated. Each empire, for reasons of expedience more than benevolence, protected the Jews in two basic ways: by defining the position of the Jews as a distinct group within the empire, and by creating conditions in which the inhabitants of the empire were secure, for a time at least. If Hebrew implicitly subverts imperial rule, it also soberly accepts the necessity for social stability. Its literature is not just despite imperial rule but also thanks to it.

Each empire and each form of Jewish adaptation to imperial rule differed one from the other, at times radically. Hebrew language and literature in each period were made up of a highly distinct mix of tradition and revolutionary innovation. Yet, the coincidence of historical crisis and the growth of Hebrew in four of its main periods prior to 1948 argues strongly that Hebrew has also inadvertently been an unusually sensitive antenna of global upheaval. Consistent with the history of Hebrew is the fact that since the 1939–45 war, in an age of overwhelming changes and dangers, Hebrew has grown more than it did in the three thousand years of its previous existence. It is no longer the creation of a minority religion in a foreign, often hostile, empire. Independence has diminished as well as enriched it. There are more Hebrew speakers, writers and books than ever, but these are concentrated mostly in the State of Israel. Hebrew literature since 1948 is the complex voice of a modern state, independent of empires for the first time in 2,000 years. Hebrew creativity in the diaspora has virtually died out in the process of being violently transplanted into the land of its birth.

Still, it might be pointed out in conclusion that Israeli literature is best understood in the context of its ancient development under imperial rule. As in photographs showing the outlines of Roman roads and camps, the main links with the past can still be discerned in current Hebrew literature: the intense social conscience of the prophets and their readiness to go against the current; the creative tension between neo-aggadic imagination and the rule of law and justice as in the Talmud; the highly refined aesthetics of medieval Hebrew; the willingness to face the worst in human nature and believe in the best, as in Hebrew under Tsarist rule; and in general, the commitment to the betterment of mankind and to the capacity of the human spirit to endure and to prevail.

1 Hebrew Prophecy and the Negation of Empire 750–500 BCE

Hebrew prophecy and much else in the Bible was a product of the two and a half centuries from 750 to 500 BCE,* the historical juncture when the centre of civilization was about to be wrenched from the Near East to Europe.[1] Hebrew prophecy is generally regarded as the greatest and most lasting and influential artistic creation of a powerful but dying near eastern civilization built upon imperialism and the newly harnessed technology of the Iron Age. We know of three major waves of Hebrew prophecy. Each accompanied a wave of imperial conquest, first by Assyria in the late 8th century, then by Babylonia in the late 7th and early 6th centuries, and finally by Persia in the mid-6th century. Many Hebrew prophetic poems were written in direct reaction to imperialism. They often describe specific events in the lives of empires – the fall of Nineveh in 612, for example, the battle of Carchemish in 605, or the conquest of Babylon by Cyrus in 539. Prophecy taught an alternative to imperialism, the basis of modern religion: belief in one abstract God, the only eternal imperial conqueror, demanding adherence to moral principles and laws.

Each surviving wave of prophecy is chronologically inseparable from a time of war. War is the subject of, or background to, most of the prophetic poetry, even that depicting the golden age at the end of days when swords are beaten into ploughshares and the wolf lies down with the lamb. It is often overlooked that Isaiah's idealistic vision goes on to predict a time when Israel and Judah gain resounding *military* victories over their enemies (Isaiah 11). Only then will God be 'king of the whole earth' (Zechariah 14:9). This image of imperial rule was deeply influenced, no doubt, by the Mesopotamian kings who used an identical phrase to describe the extent of their power (e.g. Pritchard, 1969, p. 297). The prophetic idea of divine power inevitably had for its chief model the kings of Mesopotamia. These kings claimed and were believed by their

*Dates in this chapter are all BCE.

28

subjects to be divine. So it is not totally surprising that the prophets' descriptions of God as imperial warrior, defender of justice, of the weak and the poor, use language which might also be applied to the image of the Mesopotamian kings:

> North from Teman, Eloah will come,
> past Paran, the Holy One.
> His glory wraps the skies,
> the earth is filled with his praise.
> Horns of light, hidden strength,
> bursting from his hands.
> Plague scorches his way.
> Fire bolts at his feet.
>
> He stops – the earth shudders.
> A glance – nations tremble.
> Timeless mountains crumble.
> Hills bow ancient heads.
> He follows their eternal paths.
> I see tents of Cushan terrified,
> Midianite curtains shake...
>
> You stamp the earth in rage,
> in anger thresh nations.
> You come to save your people,
> to rescue your anointed.
> You decapitate the house of the wicked,
> cutting its neck bare to the base,
> You pierce the heads of their rulers
> with their own weapons
>
> as they storm in to scatter us,
> happy to devour the poor, in secret.
> You tread the sea with your horses,
> mightily the waters foamed!
>
> (Habakkuk 3:3–7, 12–15)

The prophets identified the Jews with a spiritual empire, an immortal kingdom of God mirroring and rivalling Mesopotamian kingdoms with their feet of clay. In this way, they stretched the range of creative imagination and enabled their people to hold on to their unique identity even, and perhaps especially, in exile.

While the prophets extol the virtues of submission, justice, kindness and mercy, their strongest moods are of angry defiance, accusation and bitter guilt; and this might be explained in the context of imperial expansion in the two hundred years starting from the mid-8th century. It cannot be accidental that the first extant written prophecies – of Isaiah ben Amoz, Hosea, Amos and Micah – coincide with an astounding series of Assyrian conquests in the second half of the 8th century. During that time, hardly a year passed without a military campaign. The cataclysmic effect of these wars of expansion may be gauged in Isaiah's impassioned prophecies to surrounding nations – Egypt, Ethiopia, Arabia, Aram, Edom, Moab, Phoenicia, Philistia, as well as Assyria and Babylonia. The Assyrian victory over Aram in 732 called up the following lines from Isaiah:

> Damascus is a city no longer
> but a gutted ruin...
> Abandoned, the towns of Aroer
> where sheep graze freely,
> unafraid.
>
> Ephraim will lose its fortresses,
> Damascus its kingdom.
> What's left of Aram –
> like Israel shrunk,
> says the Lord of hosts.

(17:1–3)

The defeat of Tyre in the late 8th century gave Assyria control over a vital link in the Mediterranean trade routes. Tyre's location on a rock island off the coast made it almost impregnable. Assyria forced it to submit and to pay tribute:

> *Howl! ships of Tarshish*
> *for your homes are plundered!*
>
> Dumbstruck is Cyprus
> and the Mediterranean coast,
> once full of Egyptian grain,
> harvest of the Nile –
> for Tyre was market of nations...
>
> Despair, Zidon! for the sea-fortress said:
> I was never in labour,

I never gave birth,
I never raised
your young men and women...
The news will terrify Egypt.

Howl! men of Tyre:
Take refuge in Tarshish!

Is this your good-time town of old,
settling foreign lands?

Who brought this on Tyre,
 Phoenicia's crown,
whose traders were princes,
salt of the earth?

God of Hosts has done this
to pierce their pride,
to mock these honourable men.

Pour from your land like the Nile,
people of Tarshish: your harbour is gone,
nothing holds you there.

God has struck the sea,
shaken kingdoms, commanded the ruin
of Canaan's fortresses.

Howl! ships of Tarshish
for your homes are plundered!

(23:1–11, 14)

Assyria's main wars, however, were fought against Babylonia, which
it defeated no fewer than four times between 729 and 689. Here is a
poem of Isaiah's in response to one of these wars:

Terror grips me, and confusion,
this lovely evening turned to nightmare...
Table set, lamps lit, feasting, drinking –
Then –

Up princes! Oil your shield!

For the Lord had told me this:
Act as a watchman, speak out what you see!

A chariot I saw, a team of horses,
    donkey and rider, camel and rider.
I strained to hear their message,
and I roared:

Fallen, fallen is Babylon.
All her idols smashed
to earth!

O Israel, thrashed and scattered:
I tell you this
which I heard from the Lord of Hosts
God of Israel!

(21:4–9)

Isaiah's prophecies to the nations barely acknowledge Assyria as the main cause of upheaval, perhaps because this was self-evident. It might also have been a slap at Assyria by attributing its victories not to its superior power but to God. The prophecies to the nations in Isaiah and later prophets, Jeremiah and Ezekiel in particular – there are about three dozen such prophecies in all – chart the course and impact of imperial expansion and give a unique outsider's view of the great events of the age. The threat of being overrun and the experience of vassaldom helped bring about an explosion of creativity in Judah starting from the mid-8th century. Prophecy served to control and make sense of otherwise uncontrollable, incomprehensible, earth-shaking events. The prophets denied military defeat by creating works with permanent theological and aesthetic value.

Tiglath Pileser III, a general who usurped the throne around 745, was chiefly responsible for Assyria's rise as the first extended empire in history. He conquered most of the Fertile Crescent, made the northern and eastern borders safe from marauding tribes, and divided the territory into administrative units designed to protect the trade routes and to collect taxes with maximum ease. To these ends, he built a network of roads – the finest prior to the Romans – together with a chain of resting posts and forts. To ensure the disorientation of his defeated enemies, to make use of them and, finally, to assimilate them into Assyrian cities, he instituted a policy of deportation to the Mesopotamian heartland where the exiles were put to work on public building projects. This policy inadvertently had momentous consequences for civilization. It broke down ethnic barriers and opened the way for the future extension of prophetic influence and of Judaism (and through Judaism, Hellenism and, later, Christianity and Islam) as a universal religion. But at the time, deportation was a catastrophe. Israel was exiled by the Assyrians and Judah by the Babylonians, and this policy was reversed only by the Persians in the late 6th century. At this point, the prophetic age ended.

Assyria, however, had serious problems of its own, the overcoming of which through brute force made it briefly the most powerful empire in history up to that time. Geographically, Assyria had no clearly defined borders: it was surrounded on all sides by often-hostile nations and tribes. While it had much fertile land by the Tigris and its tributaries, which attracted invaders, Assyria had few raw materials and had to import wood, stone, bronze, copper, wool, flax and, above all, iron. (This economic reality may have influenced the Mesopotamian worship of idols of wood and stone, which the prophets mock and condemn ceaselessly – such commodities, plentiful to the Judeans, were precious to the Assyrians.) A further destabilizing factor was the irregular rise and fall of the Tigris and Euphrates, which could lead to inadequate irrigation one year and flooding the next, and which required an elaborate and not always effective system of dykes and canals. These conditions forced Assyria to maintain a strong army and to look beyond its borders, especially to the Mediterranean coast, for raw materials. The 8th century was a time of expanding Mediterranean trade, and one of Tiglath Pileser III's chief military feats was the conquest of the east Mediterranean coast, with its trade routes and ports. His successors, Shalmaneser V, Sargon II, Sennacherib, Esarhaddon and Ashurbanipal, were largely successful in consolidating the empire and maintaining control over trade from Egypt to Persia and northwards to the Taurus mountains. The growth of international trade increased the strategic importance of Israel and Judah, straddling the land bridge between Asia and Africa. The prophets were not wrong in speaking of their land as central.

The discovery of the uses of iron – the greatest technological advance of the biblical era – made possible the type of imperialism created by Assyria as well as the defences against imperialism, the military ones and also, indirectly, the spiritual ones of the prophets. The Assyrians were the first to create a large iron weapons industry, and through the mass production of iron weapons put these instruments of destruction for the first time into the hands of sizeable armies. Iron changed forever the nature of warfare, travel and trade, all crucial to imperialism. The phenomenal Assyrian military successes of the late 8th century, news of which came to Europe via the Greek trading posts in the east Mediterranean, accelerated the growth of an iron-based urban economy in Europe, paving the way for the rise of the Greek and Roman empires. Assyrian improvements in the design of the bow, the quiver, the shield, body armour and the chariot (making it heavier, strengthening the wheels), as well as increasingly effective battering rams to penetrate siege walls and city gates, were largely made possible by iron tools and materials. Iron played its part in military training and combat techniques, in the building of roads and new means of rapid, flexible deployment of troops, logistics and administration. The poetry of the prophets echoes with iron: soldiers on the march, horses galloping, the glint of javelins, the thrust of swords, the clang of chariots.

While Assyria built the finest offensive army to date, Israel and Judah and other nations in the Near East developed some of the most sophisticated means of defence: walls, siege fortifications, gates, towers and protective structures on the walls, and engineering, notably Hezekiah's 500-metre conduit hacked through the rock from the stream of Gihon into the city of Jerusalem (Yadin, 1963). Jerusalem was never conquered by the Assyrians, and Samaria, which in some places had walls 33 feet thick, resisted Assyrian siege for three years. Ethical monotheism and the prophets were part of these defences, strengthening resolve against the moral 'breach in the wall' (Isaiah 30:13), depicting God as the only king and warrior-protector – 'shield', 'wall', 'bow-man', 'chariot-driver' as well as a type of smith-creator, removing impurities, battering the heart of his people into new shape, using the prophets as tools and fortifications. The prophet Jeremiah, for example, is chosen by God to be a 'bronze wall', an 'iron pillar' and a 'walled city' protecting the faithful (Jeremiah 1:18, 15:20). Significant, too, is other prophetic imagery of iron: the iron axe wielded by God in leading the Assyrians to victory over his faithless people (Isaiah 10:34), the iron yoke made by God to symbolize the supremacy of Nebuchadrezzar (Jeremiah 28:14), the iron pen to inscribe the sins of Judah (ibid. 17:1). At the same time, the prophets denigrate the uses of iron in war as in idol-worship, and the iron-smith is a target of the most vituperative mockery in Second Isaiah.

The basis of these defences against imperialism was the invention and perfection of a simplified Hebrew script which made the Bible possible and, again via the Greeks, was the antecedent of the modern alphabet. Little is known of the origins of this script, but the 8th-century prophets, together with the works of Homer, are the earliest surviving literary examples of it. This script allowed the creation of a literature so powerful and alive that it could inspire religious faith and outlast any human empire.

Assyria's imperial growth stiffened Judah's will to survive. It also led to the destruction of Assyria within a century. The cruel force needed to build and sustain the empire aroused violent hatred throughout the Fertile Crescent. Demographically weak, Assyria could not hold down its huge empire. At virtually every opportunity, the subject nations, who provided much of the Assyrian military and administrative manpower, rebelled. Power was so centralized that the death of the king, who was believed to have divine authority, weakened the empire and often provided the best conditions for revolt. The seismic effects of the deaths of Assyrian kings are among the main events of the century preceding the annihilation of Assyria. They decisively influenced the course of history as well as the growth and character of prophetic poetry. After the death of Tiglath Pileser III in 727, Israel rebelled and was crushed and exiled. After the death of Shalmaneser V in 722, the western provinces of the empire revolted. Babylonia followed suit and waged a long, initially successful war against Assyria. The death of Sargon in 705 led to widespread revolt in both the eastern and western sides of the empire. The death of Sennacherib in 689 again set off unrest which Assyria this time managed to contain rapidly. The death of Esarhaddon in 669 brought civil war and wars with Babylonia and Egypt. Finally, the death of Ashurbanipal in 627 triggered a massive revolt and the collapse and disappearance of Assyria.

The prophets' response to Assyria was inherently ambivalent. On the one hand, Assyria was hated and feared as the piratical empire that had crushed Israel and come within a hairbreadth of doing the same to Judah. This empire had an enviably attractive polytheistic culture, needing little or no military coercion to impose it on subject nations. The people of Israel, for example, seem to have assimilated willingly, though they had fought hard to keep their independence. Their kingdom and faith were lost in exile. On the other hand, if monotheistic faith was to survive, the Judeans had to learn to accept Assyrian and, later, Babylonian and Persian victories as the will of God. Isaiah in the late 8th century describes Assyria as being God's agent:

Hoi!
Asshur, rod of my wrath!
My fury a stave in his fist!
I cast him at a deceitful nation
  to kill and to spoil,
    to stamp him like mud in the streets!

(10:5–6)

Jeremiah, similarly, depicts the inexorable Babylonian advance on Judah in the early 6th century as an apocalyptic fulfilment of God's will:

I saw the earth – a void,
and the heavens went dark.
I saw the mountains quake
and the hills tremble.
I saw no man, not even a bird.
I saw forest turned to desert and all its cities to ruin
for fear of Yahweh . . .

(4:23–6)

Persia is described, likewise, as God's hammer and sword in the conquest of Babylon in 539.

You are my shatterer, Yahweh says,
My hammer and sword – to shatter nations,
to break kingdoms,
to shatter horse and rider, chariot and rider,
men and women, young and old,
sheep and shepherd, ox and farmer,
noble and viceroy . . .

(Jeremiah 51:20–3)

No extended prophecies against Assyria – or, for that matter, Babylonia and Persia – are found in the period of its military successes. Isaiah has no 'burden of Asshur', neither does Micah or Hosea; and the prophecies against the nations which start the book of Amos do not include Assyria. The vivid memory of Israel's exile challenged the prophets: how to maintain a monotheistic faith strong enough to keep alive a national-religious identity in exile as well as the hope of return. The lack of unity which had led to Israel's split into two kingdoms in the 10th century was another force which, paradoxically, helped Judah to survive. For after Israel's fall, Judah had over a century to ready itself psychologically for the possibility of exile, to avoid being swallowed up like Israel. The threat of exile concentrates a nation's mind wonderfully, and the prophets' writings are the full creative flowering of this concentration.

The prophets, then, were leaders in a war against cultural imperialism. Perhaps this was initially the main reason for the writing and preservation of their teachings. (It is possible that the simplification of the Hebrew script by the 8th century came about partly as a result of the need to facilitate monotheistic teaching in Palestine.) Though they accepted submission to superior military power as a condition of survival, the prophets subverted imperial rule in a number of ways: in their attacks on the materialism and injustice which were inevitable consequences of imperialism, in their apparent lack of concern with economic realities, which may be seen as a back-handed attack on the very foundation of Mespotamian expansionism; in their insistence that the divine word was not the monopoly of priest and king in the sanctuary, but could inspire the common man, even a shepherd such as Amos; in their undying hope for the ingathering of exiles, which ran directly counter to Assyrian and Babylonian policy; in their readiness to admit defeat, to depict it graphically and to accept it as the will of God; in maintaining belief in one omnipotent God in opposition to what they saw as the paltry polytheism of Mesopotamia. 'The prophetic ideal', writes Yehezkel Kaufmann, 'was the kingdom of God, the kingdom of righteousness and justice. This was the basis of the first Isaiah's negation of war and of dominion acquired by warfare. This ideal implied the negation of world rule generally, of empire . . . ' (1970, p. 117).

The unique ferocity of the prophets' attacks on idols and idol-worship, while largely ignoring the rich mythology of pagan beliefs, derived in no small measure from the awareness that the power of idols was dependent totally on military might. Only nations with sufficient power could afford to believe in such gods, and even they would fall in the end. A nation such as Judah was too weak to believe in idols. The insight of the prophets was apparently shared by no other religious leaders of the surrounding nations: that idols were a threat to their survival. Idols could be destroyed or plundered, as happened to the gods of Israel. The fear that this would happen again drew the Judeans to belief in an invisible God. Hatred of false gods and of the magic and superstition associated with them was also inevitably bound up with the hatred of empires and of imperialism, by which the Israelites were bound to be defeated. The following lines from Second Isaiah are not just an attack on idols and idolators but also on the empires which embraced this pagan culture:

> Idolmakers are tohu –
> their precious works do no good,
> the worshippers do not see, do not know
> to be ashamed...
>
> Who in his right mind
> would make a god, melt an image –
> useless?
>
> His friends should be embarrassed,
> crimson-faced craftsmen huddled together
> should fear for him and be ashamed...
>
> Bel is bowed, Nebo bent double –
> a heavy load of gods
> carried by weary beasts
> buckling under the weight –
> They did not save a soul,
> exiles all...

> (44:9; 46:1–2)

The late 8th-century prophets were torn between detestation, hatred and fear of Assyria and identification with Assyria as the rod of God's wrath. Consequently, their hatred of Assyria was shunted to a large extent onto various targets: idols, idol-worshipping nations and Judeans who failed in moral self-discipline. With the fall of Assyria, this hatred burst out freely, without terror of reprisal. Loathing and fear of Assyrian tyranny are spelt out in the relish and horrified glee with which the prophet Nahum depicts the fall of Nineveh in 612 and of the Assyrian empire:

> Red the attacker's shield,
> warriors decked in scarlet.
> Torch-like the chariots flash,
> javelins tremble poisonously:
> Lightning torches streak.
> Chariots frenzied roar in the squares,
> the clang of steel in the streets.

Generals summoned
stumble in their march
race to the wall –
but the mantelet is moving.

Broken the river-gates,
the place floods with fear.
The queen stripped, dragged away –
her handmaids moan like doves,
beat at their breasts.
Nineveh of old was like a tranquil pool –
now her people flee in a panicked stream:

Stop! Stop!
Spoil the silver!
Spoil the gold!

There's no end to the treasure,
no end of the precious wares ...

Blasted, blank and bare:
No end of the slain.
Everywhere corpses strewn.
Mountainous dead.
Soldiers stumble on the bodies.

How your shepherds slumber,
king of Asshur!
Your warriors lie in peace.
Your people are scattered over the mountains –
no one gathers them.

There no balm to ease your pain,
the wound too deep:
All who hear of it
clap hands in glee ...
for over whom did your evil
scourge not pass?

(2: 4–11; 3:3, 18–19)

During the most stable period of the empire, from the middle of
Sennacherib's rule until the death of Ashurbanipal, from about 700
to 627, there is no datable Hebrew prophecy. It is likely that Hebrew
prophecy was suppressed, perhaps even by royal command, during

this period. Manasseh, the Judean king for much of this time,
reportedly spilt much blood. The prophets might have been
among his victims.

When the Assyrian empire collapsed in the late 7th century,
the Judeans under Josiah asserted religious independence. Josiah
began a massive reform, as Hezekiah had done nearly a century
previously in parallel circumstances. Hebrew prophecy re-
emerged. It had its second great period at a time of Babylonian
and Egyptian rivalry and the defeat and exile of Judah by the
Babylonians. The apocalyptic atmosphere of this age of military
upheaval and religious reform is captured by the prophet Zeph-
aniah:

> I will sweep the lot off the face of the earth,
> sweep man and beast, sweep bird and fish,
> idols and their devotees, from the face of the earth!
>
> I will stretch my hand against Judah
> and all the people of Jerusalem.
> I will put an end to Baal and the priests of Baal,
> the false priests of Yahweh, who worship on roofs –
> an army of gods! – those who swear by Yahweh,
> by Milcom too, those who turn from Yahweh,
> and those who never sought him out.

                                              (1: 2–6)

For a short time, Judah seemed within reach of independence.
However, after Josiah was defeated and killed by the Egyptians at
Megiddo in 609, Judah was forced back to vassaldom, under Babylonian rule. The earliest appearance of the motif of God's injustice –
why do the righteous suffer and the wicked prosper? – emerges
approximately at this time, perhaps in response to Josiah's death
and the failure to gain independence at a time of the breaking of
nations:

> If I quarrelled with you,
> you'd win, Lord,
> though I argued justly:
>
> Why do the wicked make good,
> and turncoats live in peace?

                                    (Jeremiah 12: 1–2)

How long, Yahweh, do I lament
to your deaf ears?
How long cry *Murder*!
and you do not save me?
Why do you show me wrongs,
strife, violence and ruin?
Why do you spread trouble before me?

This is why law shrivels up,
justice loses its eternal force,
why the wicked checkmate the good.

This is why justice is twisted.

(Habakkuk 1: 2–4)

The Babylonian defeat of Egypt at Carchemish in 605 left a
strong mark on prophetic poetry. The Egyptians were routed by
the Babylonian crown prince, Nebuchadrezzar. Ignominiously they
were chased south, past Judah, to the Egyptian border. This battle
firmly established Babylonian supremacy over the Fertile Crescent
and its eclipse of Assyria, which vanished from history. The poem in
the book of Jeremiah on the battle of Carchemish expresses the
Judeans' shortlived delight at the downfall of their enemy and at
being released from vassaldom. The Egyptian defeat seemed to
confirm once more God's hand in history:

This is a day
of revenge for Adonai Yahweh Zebaot!

The sword will chew up his foes,
get drunk on their blood!
This –
Yahweh's slaughter, up north
by the Euphrates.

Crawl up to Gilead,
virgin daughter of Egypt!
to find medicine;
as much as you use, it won't help –
All the nations hear your cry
and your shame
for the men of war have fallen, crashed
against each other.

(46: 10–12)

With this victory, Babylonia took over the mantle of imperial conqueror left by Assyria. As in the previous century, Judah was caught up in the jockeying for power of Egypt and Mesopotamia. The prophets warned against alliances, especially with Egypt, which could lead to moral folly and political disaster. Jeremiah was jailed in Jerusalem for his pro-Babylonian views and let go only after Nebuchadrezzar defeated Judah, burned down the Temple in Jerusalem and exiled most of its inhabitants.

Against this background, Hebrew prophecy found its most individual, sensitive and tragic voice in the poetry of Jeremiah. Jeremiah depicts his recruitment to do battle for divine truth as a painful inner struggle:

> Sorrow sweeps over me
> my heart is sick.
> My people cry out in a distant land.
> 'Is Yahweh not in Zion,
> is her King not there?'
>
> (*Why did they enrage me with their idols . . .*
> *Their foreign nothings?*)
>
> The harvest is over,
> summer has gone,
> and we have not been saved.
>
> I am broken by my people's ruin.
> I am filled with dark dismay.
>
> In Gilead is there no medicine,
> no doctor? Why are my people not healed?
>
> If my head were a store of water
> and my eyes a fountain of tears,
> I would cry day and night for the slain
> of my people.
>
> (8: 18–23)

In the book of Ezekiel, similarly, the voice of personal faith bound up with collective sorrow is an implicit challenge to the militarism of empires. The death of the prophet's wife and the destruction of the Temple in Jerusalem become symbolic of one another:

Son of Man!
I am going to take the delight
of your eyes, in a plague.
Do not lament or cry, hold back your tears.
Stifle your groans, do not mourn.
Put on your turban, put on your shoes.
Don't cover your face, do not eat the bread
of mourners...

And I spoke to the people in the morning,
And my wife died at dusk.

The next morning I did as I was told,
and the people asked me:
What do all these things mean to us?
And I replied: The word of the Lord came to me:
Tell the House of Israel I will profane
my Temple... and Ezekiel will be a sign
to you...   (24: 16–21)

Had the Babylonian empire survived for a century or two rather than a half-century, the Judean exiles might have assimilated into Babylonian society as the Israelites had in Assyria. The rise of the Persian empire saved Judah and, in effect, made possible the survival and growth of Judaism. After his defeat of Babylonia in 539, the Persian king Cyrus issued an edict allowing the Jews exiled by the Babylonians to go back to their homes in Judah. This act stimulated the third and final wave of biblical prophecy, dominated by Second Isaiah. This poetry for the first time conveys the ecstasy of vindication, of having come through, the sheer relief of regaining the territorial homeland, and the gratitude to God and commitment to his Law. As in previous prophecy, starting from Hosea, Israel is depicted as a forsaken wife whose husband, God, takes her back:

As to a wife, abandoned and grieved,
I will call you, wife of my youth, once despised.

I forsook you for a short time
but I will take you back lovingly.

Though I hid my face in a flash of rage,
my mercy opens to you
in eternal love.   (Isaiah 54: 6–8)

The Jews, having survived, alone as it turned out among the peoples of the ancient world, felt an enormous sense of privilege, specialness, responsibility and chosenness. In the course of a single lifetime, the two most powerful empires in history, Assyria and Babylonia, had disappeared, while Judah miraculously held on. From the ecstatic viewpoint of Second Isaiah and his contemporaries, the earlier prophets such as Isaiah and Jeremiah had been proved right: faith in the end was indeed stronger than military force. And so, in their desperate search for defences against imperialism, the prophets discovered an alternative to empire which became the basis of Judaism in exile and, later, of Christianity and Islam. Faith is independent of time and place – this was their discovery. They prepared the way for what Isaiah Berlin called 'a culture on wheels', a mobile culture built upon faith and viable in exile.

Most of the main elements of Judaism in exile appear to have crystallized into a religious way of life under Persian rule, at the tail-end of the prophetic period (the prophets vanished, one feels, because their task was done): belief in one invisible universal God and the total rejection of idols and magic; attachment to the memory of the Land of Israel; the introduction of synagogue worship as a substitute for Temple worship, and of prayer and study in place of the sacrifices; the repudiation of intermarriage; and the concept of the Messiah who would appear at the end of days and restore the Davidic kingdom of Judah. Precisely because in exile Hebrew lapsed into being a secondary language, it could now more effectively emerge as the sacred language of Scripture, prayer and law. Crisis, far from crushing the Jews and their religion, gave them new life and new direction.

Judaism and the Hebrew literature which served as its vehicle were the only substantial body of ancient near eastern culture to survive in the long term the shift in the vanguard of civilization from the Near East to Europe. In Hebrew, ironically, the extinct empires continued to live, but on Jewish terms: in the Hebrew language itself, much of whose vocabulary has roots identical with or similar to the ancient Mesoptamian dialects; in the Mesopotamian myths such as the flood story which had been adapted in Hebrew; in the image of God as imperial conqueror; in the post-biblical period through peaceful missionary activity. The prophets' success in creating a self-contained religious culture which could survive in a far larger and more powerful imperial culture ensured the survival of the Jews as well as the future tensions between Judaism with the dominant culture. These tensions reached a climax in the Roman empire five hundred years after the prophetic age.

2 Hebrew in the 'Evil Empire' of Rome 66–200 CE

The 'evil empire', as the rabbis called Rome, crushed and humiliated the Jews in the years 66–138 CE with a ferocity that largely determined the socio-psychological and religious character of the Jews and Judaism until modern times. Yet the Jews were not defeated in their spiritual and cultural life. To the contrary. Between the years 66 CE, when the Great Revolt began, until the editing of the Mishna around 200 CE, Judaism underwent a sea change. Judging from the surviving evidence, original Hebrew in the Roman empire blossomed in the form of homiletics, exegesis, liturgy, law and aggadah, to an extent greater than in any period between the prophetic age and the 'golden age' of Hebrew poetry in medieval Spain. In common with the Bible, this literature gives a unique outsider's image of the dominant empire by a minority whose military defeats paradoxically raised the value of its religious-literary culture.

Hebrew literature under Roman rule includes two literary forms which in style and content mark a clear break with the Bible, from which they, nevertheless, take ultimate authority:

1. The Oral Law preserved in scintillating Hebrew in the Mishna the first major code of halakhah (law) and basis of the Talmud. This work, edited by Judah Hanasi around 200 CE, is a record of Judaism as practised prior to 70 CE and, to a large extent, afterwards.

2. Historical and semi-historical stories, legends, folklore, parables, ethics and mysticism, generally grouped under the rubric of aggadah. This material was later edited into the Talmud and Midrash and tells, among other things, of the outstanding rabbis of the period 66–200 CE. These sources, though fragmented, build a remarkable literary portrait of the age.

The spiritual impetus and intellectual foundation both of Jewish law and aggadah in the Talmud and Midrash derive mostly from the first two centuries CE. Though Jewish law at this time was exceptionally creative (as was Roman law at the same time), this chapter will chiefly address the more purely literary creativity of aggadah. Many peoples suffered a fate similar to that of the Jews under Rome. None succeeded in preserving their memories of ruin and hopes of regeneration as the rabbis did in aggadah. Their brief, brilliant fragments of aggadah are the heart of Hebrew creativity in the Roman empire.

The aura of sacredness which enveloped the Hebrew Bible was extended to include the Mishna and Midrash. The words of the *tannaim* (rabbis of the Mishna) were treated as sacred by their pupils and were memorized and faithfully preserved verbatim as a religious duty, in some cases for many generations before they were written down.[1] This literature was stimulated by the growth of synagogue life and a new system of Jewish education after the destruction of the Temple. Much of it recreates the past: the Midrash (e.g. the *Mekhilta*, *Sifra* and *Sifre*) of the ancestral tradition of the escape from slavery to freedom in Egypt; and the Mishna of the time before the destruction of the Temple in 70 CE. It was used by the rabbis as a divine healing tool, to confront and master defeat and humiliation, including crushed messianic yearnings. The aching ambivalent longing to restore what had been lost, to come to terms with the loss, to retain Jewish identity and its fixities of faith in exile, to be renewed – these were among the chief underlying motives and themes of Hebrew literature of the post-70 CE years. It expressed feelings which came out of survival: diverse shades of grief together with a heightened sense of chosenness and hope for the future.

Hebrew literature of the *tannaic* age was not just a response to trauma. It reflects many currents of conflict: revulsion at the pagan world of Rome, friction with the Hellenistic Greeks, the birth of Christianity as a rival religion. All these set off flight to the consolation of what seemed to be exclusively Jewish. But Hebrew literature was also a means of Jewish integration within the empire. Deeply influenced by imperial culture, it drew strength from the strength of the empire and addressed some of the empire's fundamental problems.

How did this creative tension come about, and how was it expressed? We will explore a group of fragmentary, interlocking, sometimes conflicting, causes. These build a picture – the historical accuracy of which is rarely clear – of the conditions, motives and themes which gave Hebrew life under Roman rule.

How did Rome see the Jews? The expansion of the empire in the 1st century BCE brought within its borders the majority of the world's Jewish population, perhaps as many as 6,000,000. Less than half of these Jews are thought to have lived in the independent kingdom of Judaea (Baron, 1971, 13: 871). Rome conquered Judaea in 63 BCE and formally annexed it in 6 CE. Judaea remained under its rule for half a millennium, until the fall of the empire. It was now part of a bloc of Roman territories which acted as a bulwark against Parthia, Rome's most dangerous enemy on its eastern frontier. The Jews there were, at times, among the most volatile and least integrated people in the empire. Their privileges highlighted their unusual status: freedom of worship, freedom from army service and from emperor worship. Judaism, officially classed as a *religio licita*, was dynamic and potentially attractive to large numbers of pagans.

The extent of conversion to Judaism, adoption of Jewish customs or sympathy with Judaism is unknown. Yet, it marks out the Roman empire from the other empires studied in this book. For the Jews and Judaism were, uniquely at this time, in a two-way street of limited assimilation into pagan society and of being assimilated into by non-Jews (Gager, 1983; Feldman, 1993). Imperial crisis was a contributory cause of wars with the Jews which arrested this process. Ideological anti-Semitism emerged for the first time in history as a major social and political force. The Jews were portrayed as lepers, the plague and enemy of mankind. One of the Jewish responses to defeat and hatred was a revolutionary body of Hebrew literature.

The forms of imperial crisis which corroded the Roman empire were in some ways unlike those which brought down most other empires. Rome, in fact, reached the height of its power in the middle of the *tannaic* age, during the reign of Trajan (98–117 CE). Its own historians reveal, however, that it was shaken periodically by internal discord and revolts. It was undermined by social inequity and political corruption, by spiritual and ideological weaknesses which worked slowly toward its ultimate fall. The Jews and Judaism were at times, to various degrees, seen by Rome – not without reason – as a threat to the empire's survival (Smallwood, 1976, p. 541). Anger and contempt towards the Jews were stirred up by the three Jewish revolts. These were the last, most dangerous challenge to the empire's military might within its borders. In particular, Jewish messianism was seen by Rome as a political danger. Once broken militarily and politically – symbolized by the destruction of the Temple in Jerusalem – the Jews could be let alone, to recreate their religious culture and develop the Hebrew language and literature as they wanted.

How did the Jews see Rome? Their expansion was stopped by military defeat and a ban on proselytization. They reacted to some extent as they had during the persecution of Antiochus IV in 168–165 BCE: with hatred of pagan culture and a sharp psychological turning inward. While Greek and Aramaic were used in daily life by Jews and pagans alike, Hebrew was used only by the Jews. It was unstained by enemy use. Catastrophe was a spur driving the Jews to write down oral literature based on rabbinic teachings since the time of the Bible. Their aim: to ensure the survival of the Jewish people and of Judaism.

POLITICAL AND SOCIAL ORIGINS OF HEBREW LITERATURE UNDER ROMAN RULE

The two centuries of the Mishnaic age (first two centuries CE) may be divided into three periods: (a) background; (b) trauma; (c) recovery.

Background 14–66 CE

Increasing imperial corruption and misrule and ethnic friction in Palestine and the Jewish diaspora from the death of Augustus in 14 CE foreshadowed the outbreak of the Jewish revolt in 66. This was a time of severe political and spiritual division in Jewish Palestine, between the Sadducees (the aristocracy), the Pharisees (religious leaders and their adherents), Zealots, Essenes and Christians, among others, making for an explosive, vulnerable society.

Trauma 66–138 CE

From the violent close of Nero's reign to the death of Hadrian, the Romans crushed three Jewish revolts. These lasted a total of over a decade: the Great Revolt of 66–73 CE, the revolts of diaspora Jews in 115–17 CE, and the Bar-Kokhba revolt of 132–5 CE. There followed the Hadrianic ban on Judaism in 135–8 CE and the massacre of those who disobeyed, including rabbis who died as martyrs. Judaea was systematically depopulated of Jews. Rabbis of the post-135 CE period were mostly exiles in Galilee. These blows

changed utterly the character of the Jewish people and of Judaism
and, indeed, the course of history.

The razing of the Temple put an end to the Temple priesthood.
The void was filled by rabbinic leadership and synagogue life, by
prayer, the education of children, study, preaching and mysticism.
This was where Hebrew language and literature came in. For
advanced students, much Jewish education was in Hebrew. The
core of the curriculum was Biblical literature. This constituted a
new form of Judaism, based on the Bible but with many changes and
innovations. These have survived to the present much as Hadrian's
Pantheon has survived in Rome – battered but intact. This Judaism
was sharpened and refined by the bitter but creative rivalry with
Hellenism and Christianity. Animal sacrifice, once thought indis-
pensable to Judaism, was transcended by the sacrifice of the heart:

> Israel in its land the nation of broken spirit, would now offer up
> one last sacrifice, lasting for how long no one knew, the contrite
> spirit, the broken heart alone.
>
> (Neusner, 1987, p. 18).

The failure of the Bar-Kokhba uprising choked the messianic hopes
which had inspired it. The Jews retained the power to guard the
Law, to obey and nurture it in hope of someday becoming worthy of
ultimate redemption. The massacre of the rabbis and the general
uncertainty of life in the Land of Israel gave dire urgency to the need
to write down their teachings to ensure they would be remembered.

Recovery 138–212 CE

This period far outlasted the 2nd century CE and in some ways has
never ended. In so far as Hebrew literature is concerned, however,
a distinct period may be identified from the accession of Antoninus
Pius in 138 CE until 212 CE, when all residents of the empire,
including the Jews, were granted Roman citizenship. During this
time, Palestinian Jewish intellectual centres flourished, mainly in
Galilee, and the Mishna was collected and edited.

As the eruption of Vesuvius a decade after the destruction of the
Temple preserved the bodies, the buildings and art of Pompeii and
Herculaneum, so also the cumulative blows of military defeat
engulfed Jewish consciousness with grief and rage which helped
preserve Judaism. Much Hebrew literature of the Mishnaic period
is, conspicuously or not, the work of a people in the agony of defeat

and shameful servitude, mourning irreparable losses, obsessed with minutiae of religious law and moral conduct, expounding their sacred texts in search of redemption, aware constantly of a noble but downtrodden faith and culture, which they regarded as being far older, richer and more viable than Rome's.

Though edited in a time of relative calm, much of this literature tells about the earlier periods and is heavy with grief.[2] Catastrophe is denied through continual yearning and searching for the lost independent homeland and Temple and the craving to recreate the past. The *Mekhilta* of Rabbi Ishmael, the 2nd century CE Midrashic commentary on the book of Exodus, may be singled out for its literary beauty, wisdom and feeling. It owes much of its power to the fact that while directed to a defeated people, it tells of the tradition of their escape from slavery to freedom. The core of the *Haggadah* of Passover, celebrating the exodus, reached its present form around the same time, in the 2nd century CE. Its literary qualities might, likewise, be linked in part to its topical political importance. Its exhortation that 'In every generation a man is obliged to see himself as if he came out of Egypt' is, on one level, a political statement: Do not forget that you once won your freedom and can do so again.

Midrash, in contrast with halakhah, is full of angry disillusionment with the 'evil empire,' source of pain and humiliation. Shock, sadness and despair were the fruits of defeat. It is estimated that hundreds of thousands of Jews were killed during and after the revolts. There were countless widows, orphans and other bereaved relatives. There was also widespread fear at having been 'abandoned' by God. Jewish self-blame for these defeats was the harder to bear as the main link to the divine and the traditional focal point of the expiation of sin – the Temple in Jerusalem – was gone. The dead are heavily idealized, especially the martyrs who, though believed to be resurrected in an afterlife, were still painfully absent. This grief reaction carried over in a potentially cloying, unhealthy form to the entire Jewish people and was woven into the very fabric of Judaism. The extraordinary highs and lows of Jewish existence, such as those experienced at that time, are commented on by Judah bar Ilai, a pupil of Akiva:

The Jews are likened [in the Bible] to dust and stars: when they fall, they fall to the dust; when they rise, they rise to the stars.

(*Megillah* 16a)

DEFEAT AND SURVIVAL

Hebrew literature of 66–200 CE followed the course of defeat, humiliation and limited recovery of the Jews. Defeat brought ominous signs, foreshadowing the course of Jewish history in the next two thousand years: the spread of ideological anti-Semitism, anti-Jewish riots and sadism, burnings of synagogues, desecrations of religious articles, a special Jewish tax, as well as the idea of *Judenrein* territory – Jerusalem and most of the former kingdom of Judah.[3] Rome aimed not just to crush the Jews in battle but also to degrade them to the point where they would despise themselves and cease being Jews, or at least be made impotent as a religious and political force. Hebrew became the chief repository of Jewish attempts to find strength, meaning and self-esteem in faith, to face the challenge of renewal.

Jews had been forced, on pain of torture or death, to curse and deny God, to violate their laws of purity, to eat forbidden food and desecrate the Sabbath. Rabbi Hiyya bar Abba, who lived through the Hadrianic persecution, recalled that time, 'when those who hallowed the Name were tortured with white-hot iron balls wedged into their armpits and with sharpened reeds pushed in under their nails' (*Pesikta de-Rab Kahana* 11:14, 1975, p. 214). According to a Midrash of the 2nd century CE, there was a killing field known as 'Hadrian's vineyard' stretching a distance equal to that from Tiberias to Sepphoris. The emperor had fenced this area with bodies of Jews killed at Betar, the last outpost of the Bar-Kokhba revolt (*Lamentations Rabbah* II 2,4). Thousands of survivors had been paraded in degrading victory celebrations. They were taunted, tortured and murdered in public entertainments in Roman amphitheatres in Palestine, Italy, North Africa and elsewhere. The talmudic stories of Elisha ben Avuya give sickening illustrations of how these atrocities could weaken faith. According to one account, Elisha abandoned his faith after seeing the ripped-out tongue of a fellow scholar, Hutzpit the Interpreter, being eaten by a pig (*Kiddushin* 39b).

When the Romans conquered Jerusalem in 70 CE, they displayed their power to the fullest and most humiliating extent. The details are well known. They prohibited Jewish sacrifice in the Temple area. They profaned the temple by sacrificing to their gods. They stationed in Jerusalem the Tenth Legion with the provocative emblem of a pig on its banner. The gold vessels of the Temple were rehoused in Rome in a specially built Temple of Peace – peace, by implication, from the Jews, currently seen as hostile and pernicious (Goodman, 1987). The emperor Vespasian ordered the voluntary annual tax which every Jew paid for the upkeep of the Temple to be paid to the Temple of Jupiter in Rome. This *fiscus Judaicus* marked the Jews out as a people to be exploited and degraded. It set a precedent which lasted until modern times. The Romans aimed to root out Jewish political nationalism and messianism. After the Bar-Kokhba war, they ploughed up Jerusalem and rebuilt it as a pagan city, Aelia Capitolina, prohibited to Jews. Judaea was renamed Syria Palaestina. The Romans built temples of Jupiter and of Hadrian on the site of the Temple. All this spelled one thing for the Jews: total defeat. But the overkill meant that all was not well with Rome.

THE LOWER DEPTHS

Defeat led to pauperization. In fragments of Hebrew and Roman literature, Jews appear as slaves and beggars, picking for food, squatting on waste land, distraught, diseased, abandoned. In an aggadah set in the post-70 CE years, Yochanan ben Zakkai meets a dishevelled woman picking grains of barley from cattle dung. She sees him and covers her face with her hair. 'Rabbi!' she cries, 'Feed me!' She is the daughter of one of the richest men in Jerusalem, and Yochanan had been a witness at her opulent wedding (*Ketubot* 66b).[4]

To Martial, writing after the Great Revolt, the Jews were one of many nuisances, incorrigible, importunate, driving him from Rome – 'the Jew taught to beg by his mother' (*Epigrams* 12.57.13). To his contemporary, Juvenal, they were a sign of decline: where once the king of Rome would rendezvous with his mistress, the beggar-Jews lay surrounded by the sum of their belongings – a beggar-basket and hay for bedding (or a haybox to keep food warm on the Sabbath) (*Satires* 1.3.10–16).[5]

The psychological toll was immense and longlasting. Roman terror was slow to wear off. Joshua ben Korcha, a survivor of the Hadrianic persecution, recalled sitting in a grove with a group of scholars. The wind rustled the leaves. They leaped up in fright and ran, thinking the Roman cavalry were in pursuit (*Sifra* on Leviticus 26:36). A stock phrase in rabbinic literature is 'With the destruction of the Temple...': for example, drought prevailed (*Ta'anit* 19b);

meat lost its flavour and the joy of sex was lost (*Sanhedrin* 75a); each day was a curse (Mishna *Sotah* IX 12); and prayer was no longer accepted in heaven (*Berakhot* 32b). Defeat to some Jews seemed to confirm the general mood of pessimism and futility in the empire. The struggle to keep the faith is reflected in the following anecdote:

> The schools of Shammai and Hillel debated two and a half years: one school argued that it is better not to be born, the other that it is better to be born. Their decision: it is better not to be born, but as man exists he should be sin-fearing.
>
> (*Eruvin* 13b)[6]

The Jews confided their suffering and scars in Hebrew laws, legal discussions and *aggadot*: for example, in laws concerning circumcision or putting on *tefillin* in secret in the fields, hiding the knife and the *tefillin*, blowing the *shofar* undetected in a pit. These otherwise puzzling laws are set against the late Hadrianic period when Judaism was banned. Other laws, many of which are preserved in Mishna *Avodah Zarah*, trace clearly the sad history of the Jews from Nero to Hadrian and a stiffening of their animosity towards Roman life and gentiles in general. Gentiles are stereotyped as murderers and rapists. Jews are prohibited from entering stadiums, circuses and arenas: here their people were murdered. They are prohibited not only from selling gentiles weapons, but also lions and bears: these were used in Roman 'entertainments'. Animals belonging to Jews must not be kept on the premises of gentile inns: gentiles are suspected of bestiality. Jewish midwives cannot suckle gentile babies: these would grow up to be idol-worshippers. And so on. Even the rental of houses and fields to gentiles in Palestine is forbidden, to stop the total de-Judaization of the Holy Land. Such sayings as 'A man sitting in a stadium is like a murderer' or 'The best of the *goyim* – kill!' came out of the Jewish revolts and the persecutions and massacres which followed.[7]

Aggadic literature is full of disgust at the gentile world. Even the achievements of the Roman empire are seen as selfish. One discussion of these achievements probably dates from the Hadrianic period:

> Rabbi Judah [bar Ilai] declared: 'How fine the works of this nation! They built market-places, bridges, bath-houses.' Rabbi Yose was silent. Rabbi Simeon bar Yochai retorted: 'Everything they did was for their own use: market-places for their whores, bath-houses for their preening, bridges for taxes.' Judah ben

Gerim [son of proselytes] informed on them. The Romans decreed: Judah who praised them would be promoted, Yose who was silent would be exiled to Sepphoris [in Galilee], Simeon who insulted them would be executed.

(*Shabbat* 33b)[8]

The estrangement of Jews and Romans is depicted further in Hebrew parables such as the following one reportedly told by Akiva, again during the Hadrianic persecution:

The evil empire decreed that the Jews must not study the Torah. Pappos ben Judah found Akiva teaching the Torah in public. 'Aren't you afraid of the Romans?' he asked. 'I'll tell you a parable,' Akiva replied. 'A fox by the river saw fishes flitting anxiously in the water. "Why are you running away?" he asked. "Because of the nets which men use to catch us," they replied. The fox asked, "Why don't you come up on dry land and we'll live together as our ancestors did?" "And you're meant to be the wisest of animals!" they exclaimed. "You're nothing but a fool. If we're scared in water, our natural element, how much more on dry land where we'll die." In the same way,' Akiva continued, 'if we are in danger while studying the Torah – "your life, the length of your days" [Deuteronomy 30:20] – how much more if we stop.'

(*Berakhot* 61b)

These, then, were the political and social circumstances in which Hebrew creativity became vitally important in the survival of the Jews and Judaism during and after their wars with Rome. Hebrew gave them insight, consolation and mastery. It helped preserve their will to survive. By setting them firmly apart from the Roman empire, it ensured that the Jews and Judaism would outlast the empire. Perhaps at no time in the history of Hebrew was there stronger belief that the language and its sacred literature were holy and worth dying for. In the aggadah of the martyrdom of Hanina ben Teradion, the letters of the alphabet have a life of their own apart from their physical appearance on the burning scrolls. During the ban on Judaism in *c.* 135–8 CE, Hanina was caught by the Romans teaching the Torah in public while holding a Torah scroll in his arms. His wife was then executed and one of his daughters sent to a brothel. He was wrapped in Torah scrolls, covered with bundles of twigs and with wet wool sponges over his heart, before being set ablaze. He had a slow, public death during which he was heard to say: 'If I were immolated naked, it would be hard. But as I am wrapped in Torah scrolls, whoever seeks revenge for this violation will avenge me.' As he was about to die, his pupils asked what he saw. He replied: 'The scrolls burn, but the letters fly up' (*Avodah Zarah* 18a).

Though martyrdom is at root a Jewish concept, such cases of self-sacrifice to affirm Jewish faith are, in fact, relatively rare in Jewish history. The images of martyrdom were seared into the Jews' collective identity. The authority and prestige of the martyrs – especially Akiva who might otherwise have been remembered in the aggadah mainly as a supporter of the failed messiah, Bar-Kokhba – underlie the creation of the Talmud and Midrash. (It is, perhaps, no accident that the Talmud begins with tractate *Berakhot* and a discussion of the *Shema*, Akiva's last words; by the end of this tractate, we learn of his martyrdom.) And yet, Hanina's martyrdom ironically involves the *denial* of the written word, for the scrolls are mere receptacles for the spirit.

SIGNS OF RECOVERY

Many survivors, especially those from Judaea, whose villages were totally obliterated (Avi-Yonah, 1976, p. 16), must have felt that they, and Judaism itself, had come close to extirpation and had survived for a purpose.[9] Whatever the historical truth of the story of Yochanan ben Zakkai's escape from Jerusalem during the Roman siege of 70 CE, there is psychological truth in the image of Judaism resurrected from the coffin. 'My sons,' he asks his pupils, 'take me from here. Make me a coffin to lie in.' They do so, put Yochanan inside and at sunset carry the coffin through the gate and into the Roman camp to the tent of Vespasian. They open the coffin and Yochanan steps out. He hails Vespasian as emperor. A few moments later, an envoy arrives from Rome and declares that Vespasian has been chosen as emperor. Vespasian asks, 'What can I offer you as a gift?' Yochanan replies: 'Give me Yavneh [Jamnia] and its wise men' (*Gittin* 56a–b).

The sense of dire urgency in the preservation of Judaism appears also in the following aggadah, also set during the Hadrianic terror when rabbinic ordination was a capital offence:

The evil empire decreed that the ordination of rabbis was to be punished by death, that the ordainees were to be executed, that the city in which ordination took place was to be razed and the surrounding area be uprooted. What did Judah ben Bava do? He went out and sat between two great hills, between two large towns, Usha and Shefaram, between their two limits for walking on Sabbath. He ordained five elders: Rabbi Meir, Rabbi Judah bar Ilai, Rabbi Simeon bar Yochai, Rabbi Yose and Rabbi Eleazar ben Shamua. Rav Awia added: Rabbi Nehemiah. When their enemies were alerted and came near, he called out, 'My sons! Run!' 'What will be of you?' they asked. 'I'm already as good as a dead stone.' His body was thrust through sieve-like with three hundred iron spears.

(Sanhedrin 14a)

Survival to the greatest rabbis of the age, such as Yochanan ben Zakkai, Meir and Simeon bar Yochai, meant an enhanced sense of the value and purpose of Jewish religious life and a determination to continue the ancestral tradition and language. Few Jews had the extreme optimism of Akiva who, according to one aggadah (*Sifre* 43), laughed triumphantly at seeing the ruins of Jerusalem: as the biblical prophecies of destruction were fulfilled, he reasoned, no doubt the prophecies of redemption would be too. Still, many survivors realized that they were lucky to emerge alive from the jaws of the Roman lion. Joshua ben Hananiah, a teacher of Akiva and disciple of Yochanan ben Zakkai, used an Aesop-like fable to make this point:

A wild lion ate its prey and a bone got stuck in its throat. He declared: 'I will reward the one who pulls the bone out!' An Egyptian heron stuck its beak in, pulled the bone out and demanded its reward. 'Go,' said the lion, 'Boast that you've been in the lion's jaws and survived.' So we too should be satisfied that we have been in the jaws of Rome and survived.

(Bereshit Rabbah LXIV 10).[10]

Though Bar-Kokhba was killed in 135 CE, Jewish messianic hopes did not die out entirely. They are preserved in Hebrew fragments. One aggadah, apparently set shortly after the Hadrianic period, tells of Yose ben Halafta, a pupil of Akiva and teacher of Judah Hanasi. Yose enters a ruined building in Jerusalem to pray. He meets the prophet Elijah, popularly regarded as a harbinger of the coming of the Messiah:

He [Elijah] guarded the entrance until I finished praying. Afterwards he asked, 'My son, why did you go into this ruin?' 'To pray.' 'You should have prayed on the road.' 'I didn't want to be disturbed by other travellers.' 'What did you hear in the ruin?' 'The echo of a heavenly voice like a dove moaning: "Woe to the children on account of whose sins I have destroyed my house, burned my palace, exiled my sons among the nations!"' Elijah said: 'I swear the voice says that every day three times a day. Moreover, every time the Jews in synagogues and houses of study declare, "Amen, may His great Name be blessed..." the Holy One, blessed be He, nods his head as it were and says: "Happy the king praised so well in his house. Woe to the father who has exiled his sons! Woe to the sons bauished from their father's table!"'

(Berakhot 3a)

This 'story' fits no orthodox literary genre. It dramatizes in miniature the ruined state of Jerusalem after the wars: the furtiveness of a rabbi in prayer (perhaps disguised as a gentile as Jews were banned from Jerusalem); the mystery of messianic longings, of the figure of Elijah; the hope of redemption, the pathos of God's own misery at his people's exile.

An unexpected side of this literature is its gentle charm and humour. In another aggadah involving Rabbi Yose, God has changed his hat as it were and, instead of depopulating his land, has become a matchmaker. The aggadah takes the form of an exchange between Rabbi Yose and an inquisitive Roman lady:

'How many days did it take the Holy One, blessed be He, to create the world?'
'Six days.'
'What has He been up to ever since?'
'He's been busy sitting making matches.'[11]

These fragments sparkle with consolation and hope. One of the most mysterious and exalted of these aggadot, again with a guest appearance of Elijah, identifies the Messiah not as a Bar-Kokhba type of warrior longed for prior to 135 CE. Rather, he is a bent, broken beggar in Rome, a figure reminiscent of the suffering servant of Isaiah 53, also a creation of defeat and exile. The aggadah tells of Rabbi Joshua ben Levi, a younger contemporary of Judah Hanasi some of whose sayings are included in *tannaic* literature (e.g.

Avot 6:2). Rabbi Joshua meets Elijah by the entrance of the cave-tomb of Simeon bar Yochai in Meron, in the Galilee:

> Rabbi Joshua asked, 'Will I enter the World to Come?' 'If this Master [God or the Messiah] wills it.' Rabbi Joshua was startled: 'We're the only ones here, but I just heard a third voice ... When will the Messiah come?' 'Go, ask him yourself.' 'Where is he?' 'By the gate of Rome.' 'How can I tell who he is?' 'He sits among the diseased beggars. They bind and unbind all their wounds together, while he does each separately, saying, "If I'm called, I won't delay.' Rabbi Joshua went to Rome and found the Messiah. 'When will the Master come?' 'Today.' [The journey from Rome to Judaea generally took several weeks.] Rabbi Joshua went back to Elijah, who said, 'He's promised you and your father a place in the World to Come.' 'No, he lied. He said he's come "today" and didn't.' Elijah replied: 'He was quoting Psalm 95:7, "Today *if* you heed His voice." '

> (*Sanhedrin* 98a)

ROME AND JERUSALEM: WORLDS APART

Persecution and defeat of the 66–138 CE period saturated Hebrew literature in a muted nationalistic spirit. Much of this literature suggests that the gap between Jews and Romans was unbridgeable. It makes clear the radical, even revolutionary differences which made Judaism attractive to pagans and dangerous to Rome:

> As the empire as a whole grew more and more homogeneous politically, economically and culturally, the Jews, who had retained their ethnic and religious integrity, now began to appear as one of the greatest obstacles to complete uniformity. Under these circumstances, the hostility of local populations was easily communicated to Romans living in the various provinces.
>
> (Baron, 1952, II, p. 103).

Rome first encountered the Jews in the 2nd century BCE during its wars with the Seleucid empire, before it became a great empire. The Jews impressed Rome with their ancient tradition and their military prowess, despite their relatively small numbers, in the Hasmonean wars. Rome consequently made an alliance with them. By the 1st century CE, however, Rome ruled the entire

Mediterranean area. It struggled to consolidate its power and internal unity. By now, the totally different way of life among the Jews – their sacred texts and Temple worship, their observance of the Sabbath, circumcision and dietary laws and laws of purity, and in general, their subordination of the state of religion – could be neither overlooked nor welcomed as evidence of Roman tolerance. The Jews were not alone in being convinced of the superiority of their religion. As the empire became increasingly Hellenized, the stubborn survival of Judaism stuck out: 'While the other Oriental religions disappeared in the general religious fusion of the time, Judaism remained essentially unaltered' (Schürer, 1986, IIIi 472). What is more, the ancient sources, both Jewish and Roman, agree that increasing numbers of pagans (especially women) were finding Judaism preferable to Graeco-Roman culture (Whittaker, 1984; Feldman, 1993). Rabbinic and Roman literature both depict imperial culture as diseased and evil.

> The Roman age was a time not only of uncontrolled bloodlust but of pessimism and nerve-failure regarding the powers of man to work out his own future. The existence and propaganda of the imperial government claiming the support of the old gods, did not remove the deep-seated feeling that every man was adrift, and everything hazardous. So the presiding deity of nerve-failure was Fortune.
>
> (Grant, 1960, p. 129)

Rabbinic Judaism implicitly assumes that man need not be adrift, for he *can* work out his own destiny and need not suffer pessimism and failure of nerve.

Roman society, with its extraordinarily large number of unmarried men and woman, and its wide practice of birth control, has been described as 'fundamentally sick' (Baron, 1952, II, p. 209). The Jews, in contrast, elevated the idea of marriage as a necessary social institution, the foundation of ethical life. The Jewish stress on religious education and laws of purity was decisive in alienation from Rome.

It would be unfair to contrast too sharply Rome's concrete practicality and gift for organization and Jewish spirituality and inspiration as the chalk and cheese of the Hellenistic and Roman imperial age. Socrates, Plato, Aristotle and other classical Greek thinkers and writers who were an essential part of a Roman aristocrat's education had a moral vision in some ways comparable with that of the rabbis. But the ideals of Greek philosophy did not always square with everyday life in the empire, which large numbers of its population experienced as materialistic, exploitative and brutal.

In a remarkable and telling historical coincidence, the Jews invented the idea and practice of martyrdom in the second century BCE around the same time that Rome invented concrete, its most lasting contribution to architecture (Ward-Perkins, 1977, p. 97).

Judaism denied material gods and the value of purely material existence in favour of spiritual ideals taught by rabbis whom they followed by consent. The Jews believed fervently in one invisible God, were intolerant of pagan gods and suspicious of gentiles. The Romans were tolerant of provincial idolatry and encouraged its syncretism into a single imperial religion. The Romans – and before them the Hellenistic kingdoms – tried to unify the empire through emperor-worship. If the emperors had been models of virtue, their claim to divinity might have been credible, at least in a metaphoric sense. But until the Antonine emperors, they were for the most part seen as murderers, sadists, sexual perverts, sybarites or madmen. Caligula's attempt to set up a statue of himself as deity in the Temple of Jerusalem was foiled by his assassination in 41 CE but, as Tacitus in his *Annals* points out, 'there remained fears [among the Jews] that a later emperor would repeat it' (XII: 54).

Repelled by the corruption of the gentile and Jewish worlds, a Jewish sect created one of the earliest organized monastic retreats in the parched waste of the Dead Sea. The Romans spread the Hellenistic virtues of civic life throughout the empire by means of a programme of public building – the forum, the market-place, the bath-house, the amphitheatre, the gymnasium – again, with the aim of achieving a unified culture. There was a sharp contrast, again, between the Greek *polis* (and later Roman *colonia*) and the notion of Jewish community (Millar, 1993, p. 352).

The Jews attached unusual value to human life. Recoiling at the cheapness of life in the empire, the rabbis showed extreme reluctance to use the death penalty, even when justified. Witnesses in capital cases were admonished in a most extraordinary way and exhorted to recognize the uniqueness of every human being:

> This is why God created Adam alone: to teach that one who kills a single human being [some versions have: a single Jew] is regarded by Scripture as having murdered an entire world, and one who saves a single person is regarded by Scripture as having

saved an entire world... The King, the King of Kings, the Holy One, blessed be He, created every man in Adam's image yet no one resembles the other – therefore, everyone is obliged to say: 'The world was created for me. This is why Adam was created alone... to keep the peace, so that no one can say to another: My father is greater than yours.'

(Mishna *Sanhedrin* 4: 5)

It may be that the Jews were humanized by suffering, weakness and self-interest. They rarely had power to hurt as Romans did. When they had power, during the rule of the Hasmoneans, they were at times brutal with their hostile neighbours and instituted a limited policy of forced conversion of the Itureans of Lebanon and Idumeans to Judaism. During the Great Revolt they massacred one another. In their last period of independence prior to modern times, 132–5 CE, Bar-Kokhba reportedly persecuted the Christians for not accepting him as their messiah.

But the Jews had neither the power nor the tradition, the need or the inclination to create a way of life comparable in its brutality to the everyday life of many, if not most, gentiles. The attractive optimism and humanism of Judaism – Jewish law, for example, prohibited infanticide, a common practice in Roman society – were more conducive to its survival and growth under imperial rule. These qualities may have struck a deep chord among some gentiles and were seen as a threat to the status quo. The Roman empire was the largest and most exploitative slave society in history.[12] Slavery existed in Jewish society as well but not on the same scale. Jewish law opposed the abuse of slaves and tended to eliminate slavery.

In the free 'entertainment' provided by the emperors in amphitheatres throughout the empire, hundreds – on some occasions, thousands – of human beings slaughtered one another on a single day in front of huge bloodthirsty crowds. This lifestyle was totally contrary to Jewish beliefs, as Josephus points out (*Antiquities* XV, 8, 1). The rabbis approved of one arena – the Torah. Its entire teaching as summed up by Hillel was: 'What is hateful to you, do not do to others' (*Shabbat* 31a). The epitaph often found for slaves and gladiators – 'I was not. I was. I shall not be. I do not care' (Whittaker, 1984, p. 210) – may be contrasted with humanitarian Jewish views such as that of Akiva: 'Beloved is man, created in God's image' (*Avot* 3: 14).

The cruelty pervading the empire, especially towards its slaves, made even Seneca's revolting *Tyrestis* seem mild. Written towards the end of Nero's reign, shortly before the Great Revolt, *Tyrestis* is the archetypal revenge drama, a story of the jealous king Atreus who murders his brother's children and serves them up for supper. An incident in Rome around the time this play was written and recorded by Tacitus (*Annals* XIV, 42–5) illustrates the sadism of imperial rule and, by extension, the attraction of Judaism. In 64 CE, the Roman Senate approved the killing of an entire household of four hundred slaves after one of these slaves murdered his master. These executions were legal in Roman law. Still, it is not hard to imagine some of the family and friends of these slaves turning to Judaism or to Jewish customs – or to Christianity – partly for the consolation of a humane religion which reduced and humanized slavery, and partly in protest against the inhumanity of imperial culture.

Many pagans were revolted and felt tainted at times by the empire. These might have been drawn to Judaism – which saw gentiles as intrinsically impure (Alon, 1977, p. 179) – as a means of purification. 'The separateness of the Jews in itself proved attractive to some pagans' (Goodman, 1996, p. 780). The *Alenu* prayer, thought by some scholars to date from the *tannaic* period, expresses a hope which some pagans may have come to share, in a time 'when the world will be perfected [lit. "repaired"] under the kingdom of the Almighty, and all people will call upon your name'. Charity – a uniquely Jewish custom prior to the rise of Christianity – would also have drawn downtrodden pagans to Judaism.

Conversion to Judaism or the adoption of Jewish customs had many possible causes. One of these was undoubtedly the widespread smouldering hatred of imperial rule. Judaism, though a *religio licita*, was generally despised by the Roman ruling class as a foolish, barbarous superstition. The underprivileged, powerless, persecuted classes of the empires – the vast majority – could express hatred and protest indirectly through identification with a religion and a people that, despite military weakness, confronted the empire: in its refusal to worship the emperor; in its reluctance to assimilate; in its faith in an eternal, omnipotent 'kingdom of heaven' beside which imperial rule was evanescent; in its insistence on the supreme value of human life and of moral education; and in general in its perceived capacity to fill the spiritual vacuum in Roman religion. A branch of Judaism offered an alternative to – some might say a parody of – emperor-worship: the deification of the common man and attainment through faith of messianic salvation.

THE BATTLE FOR THE SOUL OF ROME

None of the differences between Rome and the Jews was in itself seen by Rome as a danger. In fact, Rome's consistency in preserving the civil rights and privileges of the diaspora Jews was a sign of the empire's tolerance. Part of the trouble with the Jews from a Roman viewpoint was that, like the empire itself, Judaism was not confined to a specific territory. It could in theory expand indefinitely: as an empire of the spirit, it was open to all. Its existence, however passive, was a challenge. Judaism by its very nature exposed the spiritual void in the empire and could be a superior magnet. 'For the spiritually hungry,' writes Jenkyns (1992), 'Roman religion had nothing to give: it lacked moral or theological content, and it was incapable of growth or adaptation; in the midst of a sophisticated, Hellenized civilization, it remained stubbornly primitive' (p. 8). There were alternatives which, like Judaism, were odious to Rome – the worship of the Persian god Mithras, for example, or the Egyptian goddess Isis, or the Greek god Bacchus; but as Fox (1986) points out, 'Much the most attractive belief was full-fledged Judaism' (p. 271). In *Against Apion* (2.39), Josephus states with pride that Jewish customs – particularly the Sabbath and the dietary laws – pervaded the empire. Even after its defeats in the Roman–Jewish wars, Judaism retained its powerful and continuing attraction in the pagan world (Fox, 1986).

Jews had apparently invented the idea of religious conversion hundreds of years previously – there are hints of it already in Second Isaiah (56: 1–8). Yet one sign of its appeal is that it was not primarily a missionary religion and did not have to be one. There is, in fact, no proof of a universal proselytizing mission in the 1st century CE to convert pagans to Judaism (Goodman, 1994). The only known Jewish missionaries were Christian. Judaism in the early imperial age, according to Millar (in Schürer, 1986), may have expanded as a result of various causes other than active mission: 1. Attempts in Jewish texts in Greek to present Judaism in a form acceptable to gentiles; 2. The practical direction of Jewish religion, which was more definite and comprehensive than pagan religion; 3. The openness of Graeco-Roman paganism to influences of new cult forms, including Judaism (IIIi 155). Consequently, large numbers of gentiles attached themselves to Jewish communities, took part in Jewish divine service and observed Jewish precepts (*ibid.* pp. 160–1). (It is likely, however, that especially before 70 CE, Christian missionary activity was generally seen as Jewish.) The most famous known case of conversion to Judaism during that period – that of the royal house of Adiabene – evidently came not in response to mission but out of conviction. This was true of other cases as well, for example in Antioch, Damascus and Alexandria. Despite Jewish separatism and suspicion of gentiles, and anti-Jewish propaganda, Judaism gained converts, adherents and sympathizers. These successes could also be felt by gentiles as a threat (Gager, 1983, p. 59), and a source of resentment (Feldman, 1993, p. 293) and of anti-Semitism (*ibid.* p. 303).

Rome and Jerusalem were capitals of rival kingdoms, one political, the other spiritual. Their respective fates in the early 60s CE pointed to violence. The Temple in Jerusalem – one of the most splendid buildings in the ancient world – was the focal point of Jewish religious and national distinctiveness and of potential proselytization, as well as of much anti-Jewish feeling. On its completion in 64 CE it reached the height of its international prestige. In that year, about two-thirds of the city of Rome burned down in the Great Fire: Judaeo-Christians were blamed. (At that time, Christianity was still a Jewish sect, and Christians were regarded by gentiles as Jews.) To the anti-Jewish elements in the Roman empire the immense prestige of the Temple at this moment may have become intolerable alongside the drastic loss of prestige and the blow to Roman morale caused by the Great Fire (and compounded by Nero's antics and monstrosities).

Apart from this, Jewish efforts to get political support and sympathy in their longstanding rivalry with Greeks, especially in Alexandria and Antioch, could easily be misinterpreted, perhaps wilfully, as evidence of proselytizing zeal, arousing enmity. Jews in some cases might have crossed the border into active mission. The estimate that Jews comprised as many as 10 per cent of the empire's population – about eight million (Baron 1952, I, p. 170; 1971, 13: 870) – attributes this expansion in part to active proselytization. Whether this was true or not, there is no doubt that – as in prejudice throughout history – some gentiles exaggerated the numbers and influence of the Jews, especially as they did not make a clear-cut distinction, as Jews did, between Jewish converts, adherents to Jewish customs and mere sympathizers. Hostile reactions to Jewish expansionism in the Roman empire are consistent with the later history of mission (e.g. Latourette, 1938–47; Stanley, 1990): societies whose cultural identity is weak, divided or insufficiently defined, and with large numbers of people on the margin, are most vulnerable to mission and, therefore, likely to fight it. Feldman (1993) has pointed out that in the history of Roman–Jewish relations, 'the question of conversion to Judaism was the single most important issue pertaining to Jews on which the emperors, both in the East and in the West, legislated' (p. 442).

Rome was not opposed to Judaism *per se* but to any potential challenge to its pre-eminence and its power to impose unity and enforce obedience. (Trajan once prohibited the creation of fire brigades on the grounds that firemen would use their right to gather as a cover for subversive activities [Pliny, *Letters*, X, 33–4].) The attraction of Judaism – whether or not stimulated by missionary activity – raised the spectre of imperial chaos.

It is likely that this fear was especially strong in Rome among the Greek freedmen who, from the time of Claudius, largely controlled the government bureaucracy (M. Aberbach, 1966). The extent of their political clout varied, but under some of the weak emperors who succeeded Augustus, 'they became the omnipotent rulers of the world limited only by each other' (Duff, 1957, p. 157). They were not, to put it mildly, enamoured of Jewish competition for the soul of Rome and naturally favoured Greeks and Hellenized Syrians against Jews.

Goodman (1996) stresses how exceptional was Roman hostility towards Judaism which led to the wars of 66–73, 115–17 and 132–35 CE:

> Such wilful hostility towards, rather than simple ignorance of, the native culture of a subject people was not typical of Roman provincial administration. It resulted in the two great Judaean revolts of A.D. 66–70 and 132–5, and in the no less sanguinary conflicts in the diaspora in A.D. 116–17. (p. 781)

Roman hostility to Jews and Judaism was political, not racial, in origin: 'official governmental prejudice against Jews was not a significant phenomenon in the ancient world' (Feldman, 1993, p. 106). However, in the course of the 1st century CE Roman attitudes towards Jews came increasingly under the influence of Greek racial anti-Semitism, which was far greater and more irreconcilable

(Gager, 1983). According to Moshe Aberbach (1966), the imperial freedmen became a primary conduit for Greek anti-Semitism in Roman policy towards the Jews. This policy created an elective affinity for the misrule of Judaea and friction between Jews and Greeks in Palestine and the diaspora. Even if Rome did not aim to provoke Jewish revolts, its actions suggest palpable designs for such provocation. Schürer condemns the Judaean procurators: 'It might be thought . . . that they all, as if by secret agreement, systematically and deliberately set out to drive the people to revolt' (1973, I, p. 455). However, the procurators did not decide imperial policy but rather were Rome's executive agents, in some cases following orders of imperial freedmen.

Among specific instances of anti-Jewish bias attributed to imperial freedmen are: (a) The above-mentioned attempt in *c.* 40 CE to set up a statue of Caligula in the Temple which, Philo writes (*Legatio* 30), was suggested to the emperor by his freedmen Helicon and Apelles; (b) The reversion of Judaea from client-kingdom under Agrippa I to procuratorial government in 44 CE, which according to Josephus (*Antiquities* XIX 9, 2 [362]) was the result of the influence of the imperial freedmen on Claudius; (c) The appointment of the ex-slave Antonius Felix as procurator of Judaea from c. 52–60 CE. He evidently reached this position partly through the influence of his brother, the imperial freedman Pallas (Smallwood, 1976, pp. 268–9). Under Felix, Judaea sank into anarchy; (d) The annulment of Jewish citizenship rights in Caesarea (*c.* 59 CE) which was reportedly the result of the freedman Beryllus' intervention with the emperor Nero (*ibid.* XX 8, 9 [182]).

Anti-Jewish bias of the imperial government might be seen as the smoking gun of a more widespread fear, especially among Greeks, that monotheistic Jewish civilization could prove to be more powerful than the Hellenistic culture adopted by the empire. The misrule of Judaea was unusual in an empire which prided itself on its unprecedentedly effective administration almost everywhere else: 'this is to be your skill,' Anchises tells his son Aeneas, founder of Rome, in Virgil's *Aeneid*: 'to graft tradition onto peace' (6:852–3).[13] This is an idealistic Roman self-image. Even so, it might be asked in the case of Judaea: why was provocation grafted onto oppression, humiliation onto anarchy?

Sporadic, though consistent, Roman hostility towards Jews, as well as its misrule of Judaea, might be explained partly by the fear that Jews were swamping the Hellenistic cities of the empire and that

Judaism, increasingly attractive and confident, was subverting progress in the empire toward cultural and political unity. In the years prior to the 66 CE revolt, it was evidently in Rome's interests to suspend in some measure its policy of tolerance and fight these trends. Hostility and misrule in reaction to Jewish expansionism combined with weaknesses in Judaean society (mostly caused or exacerbated by Roman rule) to set off the 66 CE revolt:

> The anti-Semitic Seneca government may have approved – if not openly, at any rate secretly – the provocative and hostile policy pursued by Felix as a step toward the ultimate liquidation of the Jewish state, source of Jewish proselytizing activities (M. Aberbach, 1966, p. 45).

In the generation or so before the 66–73 CE war, Rome and its Hellenistic supporters have been most troubled by the contagious nature of Jewish visions of redemption as a symbolic call for liberation from Roman rule. Such visions had begun to spread within pagan society in the mid-1st century CE.[14] Horace's famous description of Greece – 'Graecia capta ferum victorem cepit' (Greece, once overcome, overcame her wild conqueror: *Epistles* II i 156) – seemed increasingly true of the Jews *vis-à-vis* Rome. Seneca is reported by St Augustine in *City of God* (6, 11) to have said as much about the spread of Judaism through the empire in the 1st century CE: 'Victi victoribus leges dederunt' (The conquered have given laws to the conquerors).

Nominally neutral politically and officially recognized as such, Judaism was a tinderbox in the empire. Most radical was the teaching that one could not serve both God and Caesar, and that revolt against Rome was a religious duty. The hope for independence from Rome was not confined to extremists. It was a religious imperative of Judaism (Goodman, 1987, p. 12). The popular appeal of Judaism, with its visions of the 'kingdom of heaven' to be achieved with the coming of the messiah, threatened imperial rule:

> Once Palestine was annexed [in 6 CE], conversion had political overtones which might be dangerous, since the Jews formed a national as well as a religious unit, and there was possibly a fear in the Roman mind that religious adherence might involve active sympathy for anti-Roman sentiment in Palestine ... In Palestine the Jewish religion was not a harmless racial eccentricity but a

politically subversive force from the viewpoint of Rome as the occupying and governing power, because it was inextricably bound up with the nationalist aspirations which sprang from militant Jewish messianism.

(Smallwood, 1976, p. 541)[15]

The Jewish regimes to which the revolts of 66 CE and 132 CE gave rise were clearly nationalist, seeking the fulfilment of national traditions in independence from Rome (Millar, 1993, p. 337). Strong Jewish government might have controlled the population in 66 CE (Goodman, 1987). But in the long run, it is unlikely that revolt in Judaea could have been prevented, in the face of the inherent disparities and conflicts between the Roman and Jewish systems, Roman hostility to and provocation of the Jews, and the clear favouritism shown by the Roman government to Greeks in their rivalry with Jews.

The Great Revolt taught Rome to regard any organized Jewish political leadership as a potential nationalist threat. Rome did not re-establish a ruling class in Judaea, as it did after revolts in Gaul, Pannonia, Dalmatia, Britain and among the Batavi (Dyson, 1971; Goodman, 1987). Rome evidently feared repeated flare-ups of political messianism in Judaea which could again threaten the empire, a consideration which later determined Roman policy towards Christianity. The wholesale destruction of Judaean synagogues was, likewise, an attempt to crush at source what were then seen as challenges to imperial rule. In the end, after the Bar-Kokhba revolt, Rome allowed Judaism to survive with its hands tied: 'in return for the right to the full and free practice of their religion the Jews were to give up proselytization' (Smallwood, 1976, p. 472).

HEBREW AND REVOLUTIONARY JEWISH EDUCATION

Unable to expand outward, the Jews were forced inward, to expand their spiritual territory, a vital part of which was Hebrew literature. Prior to the revolt in 66 CE, Hebrew had been in decline for some time, having been largely superseded by Aramaic in rural Palestine and Greek in the Hellenistic or Hellenized cities. In the school of Rabban Gamaliel the Second, grandfather of Judah Hanasi, half the students reportedly studied Greek wisdom (*Bava Kamma* 83a). The survivors of the revolt were suspicious of Hellenistic culture (all the more as the Judaean ruling class had embraced it) and, to an extent, the Greek language (though many Jews continued to use Greek). 'During the war with Quietus [of 116–17 CE],' according to Mishna *Sotah* (9:14), 'the rabbis decreed that a man should not teach his son Greek.' By the time of the writing of the Mishna there was some relaxation in this attitude: the word for 'war' in this statement is not the Hebrew *milḥama* but the Greek *polemos*. In fact, rabbinic literature is full of Greek (and, to a far lesser extent, Latin) words. Still, non-Hebrew languages were generally frowned upon by the rabbis, even though they used them. Suspicion and hatred of Greek and Greek culture among the Jews increased as Greek became the universal language of the Christians and was used with great success to proselytize among Hellenized Jews. Rabbi Ishmael, a colleague of Akiva's, put Greek in a cultural twilight zone: when asked by his nephew if it was permitted to study Greek philosophy after mastering the entire Torah, he replied, 'find a time that is neither day nor night' (*Menaḥot* 99b).[16]

The decline in status of non-Jewish education after 70 CE was accompanied by the rise of Hebrew as the vehicle of a social and educational revolution. For the first time in history, the written word was put in the hands of a sizeable number of working class people. Prior to 70 CE many important Jews were politicians and warriors, such as Judah Maccabeus and Herod. After 70 CE Jewish history is dominated by masters of halakhah. As late as the time of Nero, Jewish fathers were somewhat erratically in charge of teaching their children. According to rabbinic tradition, Jewish education was systematized by the High Priest Joshua ben Gamla shortly before the outbreak of the 66–73 CE revolt: 'He decreed that teachers be sent to every province and every city and that children should begin their studies at the age of six or seven' (*Bava Batra* 21a). Social division in Jewish life was largely obliterated after the destruction of the Temple. Power passed from the Jewish kings, warriors and priests to the rabbis. The rabbis were not universally admired, nor were they a splinter group of closed, solitary savants (Levine, 1989). Many of the rabbis came from common backgrounds and had common occupations – there were cobblers, bakers, scribes, shepherds, tanners, needle-makers, smiths and even a gladiator (Resh Lakish) among them – none of which they denigrated.[17] *Sifre* on Deuteronomy 32:25 identifies the 'craftsmen and smiths' exiled to Babylonia by Nebuchadrezzar (597 BCE) with gifted scholars engaged in 'the warfare of Torah' (321).

The rabbis recognized Hebrew as a major key to social power. They made a concerted effort after the destruction of the Temple to increase the use of Hebrew not only in the liturgy, homiletics and law, but also in daily speech. The canon of the Hebrew Bible was finally fixed by the rabbis, and much of the Hebrew liturgy in use to the present day was created or took new form during this time. Hebrew became firmly established as the essential language of prayer. (The ministering angels were thought not to know Aramaic, only Hebrew [*Sotah* 33a].) Some rabbis such as Akiva (*Menahot* 29b) engaged in mystical concentration on the letters of the Hebrew alphabet with the aim of unlocking the secrets of the universe and influencing divine will. Hebrew had the power to assuage the sense of impotence and inferiority which came with defeat. In the context of the Jewish revolts, such concentration on the Hebrew letters as that of Akiva was an implicit rejection of imperial rule. In prayer, the worshipper is enjoined to concentrate with such fervour that 'even if a king greets him he will not reply' (Mishna *Berakhot* 5:1).[18] The perception of Hebrew as a tool of Jewish survival is expressed startlingly by *Sifre* on Deuteronomy 11:19, where the failure to teach one's son Hebrew is a form of (spiritual) infanticide: 'as soon as an infant starts to talk, his father should speak to him in Hebrew and teach him the Torah. If he does not, it is as if he has buried him (46).'

Hebrew prior to 70 CE had evidently been 'kicked upstairs' to an elevated liturgical status and underuse in everyday life. Though it did not supersede Aramaic among the masses and Greek among the educated class, the use of Hebrew after 70 CE was extended to all areas of existence, including the bath-house. for which a special ruling was needed: 'It is permitted to speak of worldly things in Hebrew in the bath-house' (*Shabbat* 41a). The example of Judah Hanasi might have had a substantial influence in colloquial Hebrew usage: he insisted on speaking Hebrew at home (*Rosh Hashana* 26b). As a result, the sacredness of the Hebrew language became more compatible with its everyday use, and this too contributed to the originality of Hebrew literature in the *tannaic* age.

In the climate of war and apocalypse in the 66–138 CE period, Hebrew was recharged with nationalistic feeling: to the believer, it could speak to God, bring the Messiah, build a new Temple. The Bar-Kokhba revolt spurred its revival. The Hebrew documents from the revolt which were found in a cave by the Dead Sea in 1960 might indicate that 'Hebrew had just lately been revived by a Bar-Kokhba decree' (Yadin, 1971, p. 124). In the post-war period,

Hebrew continued to give off an undercurrent of revolt, which could not be crushed and was in any case innocuous to Rome. Nationalist passion was channelled into education. Rabbi Hiyya, a colleague of Judah Hanasi, organized an educational system in which children whom he instructed would themselves become teachers of other children, to ensure that the Torah would not be forgotten (*Ketubot* 103b).

HEBREW, EMPIRE AND THE STRUGGLE FOR UNITY

Hebrew of the *tannaic* age signified a Jewish turning inward. Yet, at the same time, it groped for remedies to the same malaises which disfigured the body politic of the empire. 'Every distress shared by Israel and the nations,' according to the Midrash (*Deuteronomy Rabbah* II 22) 'is a real trouble.' Although the empire became in some ways more stable and humane between the Great Revolt and the accession of Antoninus Pius, the basic difficulties of imperial rule were never totally resolved. Hebrew literature could not ignore the problems of the empire as they were shared by the Jews. The revival of the Hebrew language should not be minimized as a provincial Jewish phenomenon simply because only Jews engaged in it. It should be understood in the context of imperial attempts, largely successful in the short run, to deal with crisis and unite the empire, above all through the compilation and editing of Roman law. This work was done simultaneously with the Mishna under some of the most brilliant legal minds in history, such as Papinian, Paulus and Ulpian.[19]

Jewish and Roman culture of the *tannaic* age included some highly creative and daring responses to the crises of disunity and disillusionment which dogged the empire in the first two centuries of imperial rule. As we have seen, these were caused by its frequent and severe difficulties in holding down a vast, disparate conglomeration of peoples; by its brutalization of the masses through militarization and war; by its bloodthirstiness and cheapening of human life, most evident in the huge public displays in arenas and circuses in which gladiators and wild beasts fought one another to the death, and in theatres in which actors were killed or maimed as part of the performance; its failure to find spiritual unity and direction and its resort to emperor-worship; and its pessimism as to man's power to determine his future and its adoption of a philosophy of fate and

chance: 'Eat and drink now, for tomorrow we die.' The dark side of
the Roman empire threw into relief the attractiveness of Judaism
and – once Jewish proselytization was prohibited – ensured the final
victory of Christianity.

In this broader context, Hebrew literature under Roman rule
might be seen as complementary also to the outstanding works of
Latin writers. The most gifted surviving Roman contemporaries of
Yochanan ben Zakkai and Akiva were, significantly, those who wrote
in protest – the satirists Juvenal and Martial and Tacitus whose
histories comprise one of the most remarkable expressions in world
literature of disillusionment with abuse of power and lust for power.
His portrayal of Rome is one of chronic corruption, instability and
evil: 'The story upon which I embark,' writes Tacitus in the introduction to his *Histories*, covering the last third of the 1st century CE,

> is one rich with disaster, marked by bitter fighting, rent by treason,
> and even in peace sinister. Four emperors perished violently.
> There were three civil wars, still more campaigns fought against
> the foreigner, and often conflicts with combined elements of both.
>
> (I, 2)

Tacitus saw the Jews as a dangerous, divisive force, and the
spread of their customs as a threat to the empire. But only on the
surface did the Jews appear to be one unified people. The credo of
Judaism, 'the Lord is God, the Lord is One', with which dying
martyrs such as Akiva sealed their faith, was a spiritual blow to
Rome. It declared that the Jews knew who they were and what their
purpose in life was, which the empire did not. No other people in
the empire, except for Christian martyrs, showed this readiness to
die for beliefs. In fact, the disunity which plagued the empire was
mirrored among the Jews prior to the destruction of the Temple.
Baron's description of Judaea on the eve of the Great Revolt applies
almost word for word to Rome:

> By growing too fast it had absorbed too many alien elements,
> physically and culturally, made too many compromises, and
> flirted with too many alien ways of life and thought. The results
> were those sharp sectarian and political divisions which had
> almost brought it to the brink of extinction.
>
> (1952, II, p. 129)

Rome achieved a form of social electrolysis: it destroyed the
Sadducees, Essenes and Zealots, about whom nothing is heard

from soon after 70 CE; indirectly, too, it helped split Christianity from Judaism. Rome allowed only Pharisaic Judaism to survive and grow afresh as mainstream rabbinic Judaism. As Schürer put it: 'It was, in effect, precisely the annihilation of Israel's political existence which led to the triumph of rabbinic Judaism' (1973, I, p. 555). The Jews would never have achieved such unity on their own which the Roman empire, for all its might, was unable to impose upon itself.

The Jews, all too well acquainted with the perils of disunity, echoed the Roman malaise in their writings. If there was a single overriding theme and aim both of the Mishna and of aggadah in the *tannaic* era, it was to assert a central rabbinic authority, to prevent fragmentation and disintegration in the Jewish world. This leitmotif is illustrated in a familiar aggadah set soon after the destruction of the Temple, when the centre of Jewish learning had shifted to Yavneh (Jamnia), on the coast near Ashdod. The presiding figure was Gamaliel the Second. Gamaliel's brother-in-law, the great scholar Eliezer ben Hyrkanus, was the sole dissenting voice in a debate concerning the ritual purity of a certain type of oven which had come into contact with a dead creeping creature. Eliezer argued – and the heavenly powers evidently agreed with him – that the oven was pure. The entire school disagreed with him as mystical evidence was inadmissable in Halakhah. The melange of history, legend, law, homily, poetry, social criticism, moralizing, theology, humour and absurdity which enter this debate is characteristic of the best of aggadah:

'This carob-tree will prove I am right!' The tree uprooted itself and flew fifty yards. They said: 'You can't prove a thing from a flying carob-tree!' 'This brook will prove I am right!' The water turned round and flowed upstream. They said: 'You can't prove a thing from a brook!' 'These study-house walls will prove I am right!' The walls began to lean and fall when Rabbi Joshua ben Hananiah told them off: 'If scholars argue over *halakhah*, it's none of your business!' In honour of Rabbi Joshua they didn't fall, but in honour of Rabbi Eliezer they didn't straighten out either. To this day the walls are leaning over. 'The heavens will prove I am right!' Rabbi Eliezer declared. A voice sounded from heaven: 'Why do you scholars argue with Rabbi Eliezer? Don't you know that he is always right?' Rabbi Joshua got up and replied: 'We're not interested in heavenly voices. You've already told Moses at Sinai, "Follow the majority."' Rabbi Nathan met the prophet Elijah and asked: 'How did the Holy One, blessed be He, respond to all this?' Elijah replied: 'God laughed, saying, "My sons have defeated me!"'

(*Bava Metziah* 59b).

The sensitive reader might guess at the satisfaction which this aggadah gave the rabbis. Having failed to defeat the Romans in combat, the Jews overcame God in argument, and God loved them the more for it. God's sympathy is with the spirit of diversity and individualism represented by Rabbi Eliezer, but *unity* was a condition of Jewish survival after 70 CE. Eliezer's dissenting spirit – expressed also in his hate and distrust of gentiles, in his allegedly Christian sympathies and in his opposition to the standardization of prayer – led to his excommunication.[20] When Akiva broke the news to him, Eliezer wept. At this point, the aggadah goes on, one-third of the world's olives, wheat and barley was ruined, and everything he looked upon went up in flames. Meanwhile, Gamaliel was on a boat on the high seas. A storm came up threatening shipwreck. Gamaliel stood on deck and addressed the Holy One: 'You know very well that I excommunicated Rabbi Eliezer not to bring credit to myself but for your sake, that there not be many divisions in Israel' (*ibid.*). The sea calmed. Through the reluctant use of such forceful, even somewhat harsh, methods as excommunication, the rabbis preserved the unity which Rome had inadvertently thrust on them and ensured the survival of Judaism.

Rome unified the Jews by destroying those Jewish factions most inimical to its own existence, but which might well have proven fatal to Jewish survival. There is, perhaps, no better illustration than the 3rd-century rabbi Abba bar Kahana's comment on the passage in the book of Esther (3:10) in which King Ahasuerus removes his ring and gives it to Haman, in this way approving Haman's plot to exterminate the Jews: 'The removal of the ring was more efficacious than forty-eight prophets and seven prophetesses who prophesied in Israel; for all these together were unable to improve their people's conduct, but the removal of the ring did' (*Megillah* 14a). The rabbis took full advantage of the unity imposed by imperial might. They taught a form of Judaism whose implicit objective was not obedience to worldly power but to carry out the divine will as revealed in the Torah. 'Lust not after the table of kings: your table is greater than theirs, your crown too' (*Avot* 6:5). Ultimately, observance of the Law would lead to Israel's redemption and liberation from Roman rule. The fixed elements of rabbinic theology of the kingdom of God are based on the envisaged triumph of the empire of the spirit over the 'evil empire'.[21]

FROM BAR-KOKHBA TO THE MISHNA

The resurrection of Jewish life and culture in the Roman empire after 138 CE was possible only on Roman terms. Hebrew literature is misleading in its failure to acknowledge how fully its existence and development were owing to the *Pax Romana*. Synagogues and rabbinic homiletics could not have flourished in the latter half of the 2nd century CE, and the Mishna could not have been edited, without Roman toleration. It was created by rabbis answerable to and protected by the Roman government (Baron, 1952, II, p. 242 ff.).[22]

Much credit for the conditions in which this revival was possible belongs to the emperors Antoninus Pius (138–61 CE) and Marcus Aurelius (161–81 CE), both men of exceptional character, in whose reigns Judah Hanasi grew from early childhood to middle age. Edward Gibbon, in *The Decline and Fall of the Roman Empire*, greatly exaggerated when he called their united reigns 'possibly the only period in the history of the world during which the happiness of a great people was the sole object of government' (1960, p. 44). Still, following the persecutions and massacres of Jews during the reigns of Nero, Vespasian, Titus, Domitian, Trajan and Hadrian, the new policies and attitudes of Antoninus Pius and Marcus Aurelius brought the Jews palpable relief.

Marcus Aurelius' *Meditations* gives a splendid character sketch of Antoninus Pius, who may have instituted the policies which allowed the Palestinian Jews to survive and the Hebrew language and literature to develop. According to the Talmud, Judah Hanasi was closely acquainted with an emperor 'Antoninus' and was probably influenced by him. It may be that this was Marcus Aurelius, especially as some of the matters discussed have Stoic content (Wallach, 1940–1). The image of Antoninus Pius which emerges in the opening of the *Meditations* (I 16) is not far removed from that which the imaginative student of the Mishna might have of Judah Hanasi, especially from tractate *Avot*. It serves as a reminder that the rabbis, in creating a literature whose primary aim was to build character and instil moral values, were not simply reacting against Roman barbarism (as they saw it) but also pursuing ideals which were part of Roman education and which account in no small measure for the positive achievements of the empire.

Warning himself against the dangers of dictatorial power to which his predecessors fell victim, Marcus Aurelius recalls the example of Antoninus Pius. Again he brings to mind tractate *Avot*, with its exhortations that time is short and that man should strive to do good, reject glory, live modestly, be aware of one's death, and be 'among the pupils of Aaron':

> Take heed not to be transformed into a Caesar, not to be dipped in the purple dye; for it does happen. Keep yourself therefore simple, good, pure, grave, unaffected... strong for your proper work. Wrestle to continue to be the man Philosophy wished to make you. Reverence the gods, save men. Life is brief; there is one harvest of earthly existence, a holy disposition and neighbourly acts. In all things like a pupil of Antoninus; his energy on behalf of what was done in accord with reason, his equability everywhere, his serene expression, his sweetness, his disdain of glory, his ambition to grasp affairs; ... his constancy and uniformity to his friends, his tolerance of plain-spoken opposition to his opinions and delight when anyone indicated a better course; and how he revered the gods without superstition. So may your last hour find you, like him, with a conscience void of reproach.
>
> (VI 30)

The advantage of sympathetic emperors was enhanced by the fact that after 135 CE Rome could not regard the Jews as a threat. Judaism ceased to be a potential large-scale missionary religion, though its attraction continued. After the Bar-Kokhba revolt, the rabbinic formula of conversion included a warning of the hazards of Judaism:

> A person who wants to convert to Judaism these days is asked: 'What is your motive? Don't you know that Israel is suffering, persecuted, oppressed, harassed and beaten down with a multitude of sorrows?'
>
> (*Yevamot* 47a)

There was no reason to maintain a ban on the observance of Judaism, the study of Torah and rabbinic discussions in Hebrew or any other language. A Roman *modus vivendi* with the Jews was politic: though beaten, they were of use to the empire, and not just as slaves.

Jewish spiritual withdrawal from the empire in Galilee after the Bar-Kokhba revolt, Goodman (1983) writes, was matched by Roman indifference. Rome no longer had a military presence in Galilee. In contrast with its policy in other newly defeated territories, Rome did not encourage Romanization in Galilee. The Galilean Jews apparently refused to take part in the life of the empire. They recoiled against Greek education, particularly rhetoric, essential in public life. Roman cultural imperialism in the 2nd century CE was in any case on the wane. These circumstances facilitated a distinctly Jewish creativity.

By the time of Antoninus Pius, the empire had reached its peak in strength and homogeneity, through military force if not spiritually. Roman strategic aims altered to the Jews' advantage. The conclusiveness of the Jewish defeat served an object lesson in the empire: never again in Roman history was there a revolt of such seriousness within the empire. The most dangerous military threats lay beyond the boundaries of the empire, among the Parthians in the east and the German tribes in the north. Widespread plague during the reign of Marcus Aurelius was another levelling influence on Romans and Jews, a reminder of the common frailty of existence. Much of the former hatred of Judaism for being different and attractive was now transferred onto Christianity which, as an illegal missionary religion, displaced Judaism as the vanguard of spiritual opposition to Rome. The Jews of the post-138 CE period could, in short, be left to lick their wounds and rebuild their lives, homes and schools, and work out their spiritual destiny with diligence.

This does not mean that the Jews totally rid themselves of hatred of Rome for past and present oppression. The Midrash frequently suggests otherwise, as in the acerbic commentary in *Sifre* on Deuteronomy 32:13, 'And he made him honey from flinty rock':

> These are the skinflint oppressors of Israel, tight as a rock. One day soon Israel will come into their inheritance and enjoy it like oil and honey. 'Curd from the herd' – consuls and generals. 'Milk of sheep' – colonels. 'Rams' – centurions. 'Herds of Bashan' – *beneficiarii* who snatch the food from our mouths. 'Goats' – senators. 'The first of the wheat' – their *matronae* (317).

Uniquely during this period, a few rabbis show appreciation of the benefits of Roman rule. Whereas Titus, Trajan and Hadrian were cursed – 'may his bones rot!' is a common imprecation – Antoninus Pius and his successors are not. In fact, the midrashic character of 'Antoninus' is consistently depicted as being sympathetic to and knowledgable about Judaism in his discussions with Judah Hanasi (e.g. Wallach, 1940–1). Rome is even complimented at times for its maintenance of the rule of law: Resh Lakish, a younger contemporary of Judah Hanasi, went so far as to interpret the passage 'and it was very good' (Genesis 1:31) as referring to Rome (reading 'Edom' for 'Adam') as Rome 'exacts justice for men' (*Bereshit Rabbah* IX 13). The rabbis were well aware that Rome's power could not only crush the Jews but also defend them from invasion. They feared anarchy and expressed concern over the, incursions of Germanic tribes and other barbarians who spread terror in the empire: 'If they break out [of their borders into the empire], they will destroy the whole world' (*Megillah* 6b). Judah Hanasi, who owned a large estate, might have regarded the Roman army, with some reservations, as a protective force.[23]

MEKHILTA, SIFRA, SIFRE

The midrashic literature which came out of Jewish catastrophe was the cumulative work of men who, in some cases, had suffered persecution and lived on the run together, and learned to trust one another in adversity. Though compression was necessary in an age when writing materials were scarce, their clipped, occasionally cryptic, almost military style also suggests a picture of men who have known one another long and well, and perhaps also the caution that comes of the fear of betrayal. Their discussions might be seen as the sublimation of a military instinct (*Sanhedrin* 111b). The fragmentation, incoherence and impenetrability of some midrashim are not dissimilar from features of emotional breakdown. A multitude of voices cry out for an answer, shoring fragments of sacred texts against ruin.

The *tannaim* used the weekly readings from the Five Books of Moses as a primary basis for their sermons in the synagogues. Some of their homilies are collected in the *Mekhilta*, on the book of Exodus; in *Sifra*, on the book of Leviticus; and *Sifre*, on the books of Numbers and Deuteronomy. This work is full of wisdom and literary beauty and may now be assessed as among the most important and revolutionary literature created in the Roman empire in the 2nd century CE. But at the time it was of little interest except to Jews. So far as we know, the Romans were largely ignorant of the nationalist power inherent in a system of teaching, prayer and religious festivals whose core image was the emergence of a people from slavery to freedom. The Jews, then, kept alive the image of freedom, in literary if not historical reality; and the historical reality could, therefore, be envisaged and potentially recreated.

Though these midrashim are formally subservient to Scripture, they display soaring flights of originality, which literary scholars have come increasingly to recognize in recent years (e.g. Hartman and Budick, 1986). A musical analogy is apt here. Rachmaninov's 24 variations on a theme of Paganini is for the most part just that: Paganini is the innovator, Rachmaninov the creator of variations which are of lesser creative force. But occasionally – in the 18th variation, for instance – the creative voice of Rachmaninov takes over, to the point where Paganini becomes temporarily a peg for Rachmaninov's genius. The poetry and style of Midrash, its grief and anger as well as the ambivalence of its political direction, may be illustrated through a commentary in the *Mekhilta* on Exodus 13:24, 'And God went with them by day':

Is this possible? For is it not written, 'I fill heaven and earth, says the Lord' (Isaiah 6:3), and 'Behold the glory of the God of Israel comes from the east, its sound like th... sound of rushing waters, the earth is lit up with his glory' (Ezekiel 43:3)? So what does 'And God went with them by day' mean? Rabbi Judah Hanasi said: 'King Antoninus used to speak in public as darkness fell on him and his sons. When he left the podium, he would take a lamp to light the way for his sons. His ministers would say, 'Let us take the lamp and light the way for your sons.' He would reply: 'It isn't that I'm short of volunteers to hold the lamp for my sons, but that I want to show how much I love them so that you will treat them with respect.' In the same way, the Holy One, blessed be He, showed his love for Israel to the nations by going before them personally so that the nations should treat them with respect. But they did not. Instead, they cruelly put the Jews to death. For this reason it is written: 'And I will gather all the nations and bring them down to the valley of Jehoshafat and I will judge them there' (Joel 4:2) – for idol worship, sexual immorality, or murder? No – but for my people and my inheritance, Israel. And it is written: 'Egypt will be waste and Edom a desert from the wrath of the sons of Judah, for they shed innocent blood in their land.' And from that day of judgement: 'Judah will be inhabited forever, Jerusalem for a generation . . . and I will avenge their blood, and I will not clear the guilty for the Lord dwells in Zion.' When does the Lord dwell in Zion? When 'I will avenge their blood'. (Joel 4:19–21)

That the artistry of this literature is often hard to recognize, though it is there, is itself noteworthy. There is little Hebrew fiction, history, poetry or drama in rabbinic writings. Elements of these genres appear, never in their own right, but instead in the context of halakhic discussion. Perhaps partly in recoil against the Graeco-Roman society that defeated them, the Jews avoided literary genres and the overt aestheticism associated with this society. Yet the phrasing of the rabbis is at times so precise and vivid, and the imagery so strikingly apt, that it is hard to imagine that some rabbis did not value these things – perhaps under Greek influence. The *tannaim* created an aesthetic as well as an intellectual standard for talmudic argument, which is not wild and formless but, in fact, carefully constructed to achieve a particular effect (Jacobs, 1984).

In aggadah, the Jews created a new art form which implicitly denies its own artistic power, whose fragmented quality reflects faithfully the inner world of the Jewish people and their perception of the age. In some ways, this literature is peculiarly modern. Writing of poetry in the aftermath of the First World War, T. S. Eliot, in his essay on 'The Metaphysical Poets' (1921) might have been describing the fragmentation and dislocation which characterize much talmudic and midrashic literature:

> The poet must become more and more comprehensive, more allusive, more indirect, in order to force, to dislocate if necessary, language into his meaning
>
> (1951, p. 289).

Jewish literature of the *tannaic* era and onward might be seen as a symptom of what Eliot called 'a dissociation of sensibility'. The Jews, having been cut off from active, independent political life, cut themselves off from the emotions which threatened to overwhelm them with defeat and humiliation. They entered, to a far greater extent than during the prophetic age, a world of inner reality. This world, based on faith and moral ideals, turned out to be more durable than the empire which had hurt it into being.

THE MISHNA

Together with Midrash, Jewish law in the 2nd century CE achieved rare intellectual and stylistic originality. The Mishna stands as a tranquil island between the Bar-Kokhba revolt and the political chaos and economic breakdown of the 3rd century which led to the collapse of the pagan empire. But it was edited in the aftershock of military defeat, probably on the assumption that chaos would come again. It is a work of the imagination, not only a legal compendium, and rather more eccentric than one would expect of a legal document. The Mishna is built upon two massive, covertly subversive illusions: that the Roman empire would soon be overthrown and the Temple rebuilt. (Indeed, from the Mishna alone, one might almost conclude that the Temple was never destroyed and that the Roman empire never existed.) Though compiled over a century after the destruction of the Temple, it is a classic literary example of a collective delayed mourning reaction. It creates the impression of 'wholesale retreat from a Hellenised environment' (Millar, 1993, p. 352). In fact, it was edited in a relatively cosmopolitan atmosphere in Galilee in which Hebrew and Greek flourished together (Meyers, 1992).

Much of the Mishna relates to a Jewish empire of the spirit in which the Temple is still standing. For example, it deals with agricultural laws involving, among other things, priestly gifts which continued to be given even after the destruction (*Zeraim*), the sacrificial services on festivals (*Moed*), civil law based in part upon the existence of the Temple (*Nezikin*), rules of Temple sacrificial services and the upkeep of the Temple buildings (*Kodashim*), and the taboos surrounding Temple cultic life (*Toharot*). The only order of the Mishna having nothing directly to do with the Temple is the one on women (*Nashim*). Even that often mentions the Temple, its priests and sacrifices. There is, however, one account of social and intellectual breakdown in the messianic age after the destruction of the Temple:

> At the advent of the Messiah, impudence will increase and prices will soar. The vine will yield its fruit, yet wine will be costly. The empire will fall into heresy, and no one will protest. The meeting-place of scholars will be given over to harlotry; the Galilee will be laid waste, the Golan made desolate. Those who live on the frontier will roam from town to town, and no

one will take pity on them. The wisdom of the scribes will decay, sin-fearing men will be despised, and truth will be gone. The young will shame their elders; the aged will stand up in the presence of youngsters. 'For son maligns father, daughter rebels against mother, daughter-in-law against mother-in-law, and a man's household are his enemies' [Micah 7:6]. The face of this generation is like a dog's face; the son feels no shame before his father. On whom then can we rely? On our father in heaven!

(Carmi, 1981, pp. 190–1)

Unusually emotive in style and content, this passage is placed suggestively at the end of the tractate describing a faithless woman (*Sotah*). This piece of creative editing calls up the biblical allegories of the relationship between God and Israel as a troubled and sometimes broken marriage which, nevertheless, survives.

The Mishna is a picture of a world through a glass darkly: as Neusner (1988) observes, it gives the reader little sense of author or of intended readers, of where and when it was written. Like the Talmud as a whole, the Mishna 'gives all the appearance of having dropped down from Heaven complete, as it were' (Jacobs, 1984, p. 22). It gives no sign that it was written in the Roman empire. It does not even clearly acknowledge the existence of such an empire. Its editor, Judah Hanasi, was one of the most important Jews of his time. As Patriarch, he represented the Jewish people before the Roman authorities. He lived in a sumptuous villa in Sepphoris, with a guard of Gothic soldiers, a personal gift of the emperor. Such details are learned piecemeal from aggadic sources, not from the Mishna. In the Mishna, the world has stopped, leaving a host of queries echoing in the air. It is characterized by a singular absence of violence, of passion of any sort, by quiet, formal dignity and calm precision and detachment reminiscent of Roman law, its seemingly monotonous legal minutiae punctuated with anecdote, the occasional aside and the brilliant turn of phrase. The sobriety of the Mishna contrasts forcefully with the apocalyptic fervour of Jewish (and Christian) writings of previous generations – such as 2 Baruch, 4 Ezra, The Apocalypse of Abraham and 3 Baruch – as if in realization that if the messiah had not yet come, it was not the end of the world.[24] Its magisterial calm belies its revolutionary character, for it violates the tradition against writing down oral law.

HEBREW, LOSS AND IDEALIZATION

The Jews did not turn inward willingly or easily accept defeat as the will of God. They hated the Romans with immense, longlasting but suppressed bitterness. In fact, long after the collapse of the empire, 'Rome' was a byword for all the wicked enemies of the Jews. Traumatized by Roman might, and highly vulnerable to feelings of guilt and inferiority, the Jews were also harassed by Christian missionaries who regarded Jesus as messiah and heir to the prophets. The Christians applied prophetic denunciations to the Jews and the visions of hope and redemption to themselves. The rabbis reacted strongly against the psychological consequences of defeat. In an age which saw the making of countless orphans, the rabbis themselves became communal fathers, loving and protective. They understood the need to be spoken to gently by a loving God, not denigrated, and were critical of prophetic diatribes against Israel (M. Aberbach, 1985, p. 281ff.).

Hebrew literature of the Mishnaic period and after expresses a degree of love and idealization of Israel as intense as the hatred and violence that the empire had turned on it. There is no literary precedent for such idealization except perhaps in Second Isaiah, itself a creation of exile and redemption. The rabbis of the *tannaic* age and after taught that the Jews, far from being a band of superstitious lepers, enemies of humanity, hated by God, as was alleged in contemporary anti-Semitic literature, were loved and favoured by God above all peoples, indeed above the angels (*Ḥullin* 89a, 91b). The world is spared from destruction for their sake (*Song of Songs Rabbah* II, 2, 3), and – at least in the eyes of the Halakhah – they are the aristocrats of humanity: 'All Jews are princes' (Mishna *Shabbat* 14:4). Consequently, as the early 3rd-century CE rabbi Hama ben Hanina asked rhetorically, 'What other nation is as powerful as God has made this nation [Israel]?' (*Deuteronomy Rabbah* II 15). As for 'the nations' – meaning the Roman empire – they are denigrated and cursed as being unclean and backward, foolish and sinful.

The idealization of the Hebrew language during and after the 66–138 CE period was accompanied by interwoven idealization of other elements of Jewish life, such as the Torah and Torah study, righteousness, the Land of Israel, Jerusalem, the Shekhinah and God's love for Israel. Modern psychology would recognize such intense idealization as an aspect of grief, a collective equivalent to personal loss, a means of dealing with otherwise uncontrollable anger and conflict, pain and powerlessness.[25]

In the rabbinic view, Torah was no mere intellectual exercise. It was a moral duty, but more than that, the only true freedom (*Avot* 6:2), the means for the survival of the universe (*Nedarim* 32a). Torah study, nevertheless, was regarded as a Jewish concern only because the Jews accepted it. In fact, it belonged to the world. According to Rabbi Meir, allegedly a descendant of converts and an illustrious pupil of Akiva's, 'even a gentile who studies the Torah is like a high priest' (*Bava Kamma* 38a). The exaltation of Torah is most stark at the end of *Nezikin*: 'a bastard scholar takes precedence over an ignorant high priest.' Here the psychological motive of study is revealed. It is not just a substitute or sublimation, but an improvement of Temple worship.

The rabbinic ideal of Jewish education, at the core of which is the Hebrew Bible, is underscored in a number of sayings attributed to Resh Lakish in the name of the 3rd-century rabbi, Judah Nesiah: 'The world endures for the sake of the breath of schoolchildren'; 'Schoolchildren should not stop their study even for the rebuilding of the Temple'; 'Every town in which there are no schoolchildren will be destroyed' (*Shabbat* 119b). There is piquancy in these sayings quoted by the ex-gladiator who discovered in school education the strongest weapon of all against the evils of empire.

The idealization of Hebrew and of the Land of Israel were linked. In the opinion of Rabbi Simon, a 3rd-century pupil of Joshua ben Levi, Hebrew was the holiest of languages, the language in which God created the world (*Bereshit Rabbah* XVIII, 4). Rabbi Meir, a scribe, tells how his teacher, Rabbi Ishmael, warned him that an error in this sacred work could destroy the world (*Eruvin* 13a). The Land of Israel, similarly, was the holiest of all lands (Mishna *Kelim* 1:6). In the aftermath of defeat, many Jews were deported in chains from their land. Many others were driven away by terror, famine or poverty. These circumstances underlie such views as that attributed in Sifre (333) to Rabbi Meir: 'Everyone who lives in the Land of Israel, recites the *Shema* morning and night and speaks Hebrew – is assured of the World to Come.'[26] Other sayings are in a similar vein: 'Whoever lives in the Land of Israel is regarded as a God-worshipper...And whoever lives outside the Land of Israel is regarded as an idol-worshipper' (*Ketubot* 110b); 'Those who die outside the borders of the Land of Israel will not be resurrected' (*ibid.* 111a). Jerusalem, perhaps because it was destroyed and banned to the Jews, was in the rabbinic imagination the most beautiful city in the world, if not as a physical entity then on the spiritual plane (*Kiddushin* 49b, *Ta'anit* 5a).

It is hard to tell how much of this idealization was actually believed to be true and how much was consciously an oriental exaggeration. Sublime as religion and literature, it betrays an emotional malaise which modern Zionism has reacted against. Nevertheless, the creation of what might be called Hebrew Romanticism – the yearning for a lost land and way of life – has had over the centuries a decisive impact on Jewish life and on the rise of Zionism.

HEBREW AND STOICISM

The movement toward recovery from defeat in the 1st century CE and after may be seen in the degree to which Hebrew literature of the period has parallels with – and might be influenced by – Stoic philosophy. Stoicism existed already in the biblical age but by the time of the *tannaim* became the prevalent philosophy of the upper classes throughout the Roman empire.[27] The most profound and enduring monument to Stoicism, Marcus Aurelius' *Meditations*, was written roughly in the same period as the Mishna. There are many parallels between Judaism and Stoicism (Hengel, 1981; Feldman, 1993), not least because Stoicism deals with moral questions which are central to Judaism and is, therefore, closer to Judaism than any other philosophy in the ancient world. Lieberman (1963) points out that many of the fundamental teachings of Stoicism appear in some form in the Bible. Whatever the influence of Stoicism on rabbinic Judaism, there is little doubt that certain ideas associated with Stoic thought appear more frequently and intensely during and after the *tannaic* era than previously.

The defeated Jews in the age of Antoninus Pius and Marcus Aurelius were unusually susceptible to Stoic ideas though, as always in Jewish tradition, in a disguised form assimilated into Judaism. In any case, to refrain from imitation, according to Marcus Aurelius (VI 6), is the best revenge. The aims of Stoicism were: to live with sorrow, disappointment and misfortune; to renounce worldly things; to attain calm imperturbability; to continue to believe in providence and in one universal God unconfined by temples. The Stoic has faith in the essential goodness of the world and the purpose of existence, in the virtue of good citizenship achieved through reason and good deeds, and in the intrinsic value of this study of the art of living. This philosophy was tailor-made to Jewish needs after 138 CE, and it corresponds in practically every detail with some facet of rabbinic teaching. Hebrew, with its aura of protective holiness, was itself a means of stoical resignation to the will of God.

The Stoic ideal of the Brotherhood of Man – though in practice slaves, women and Jews were mostly excluded – as well as the idea that personal suffering can be assuaged by the awareness of being part of a Whole, might have influenced the thinking of the rabbis. Rabbi Judah ben Shamua lived through the Hadrianic persecution. Acting on the advice of an influential Roman matron, he organized a night-demonstration in Rome to protest anti-Jewish decrees, presumably those passed by Hadrian. This protest brings to mind both Stoic and biblical ideals (e.g. Malachi 2:20):

> 'Are we not children of one father and one mother? Are we different from any other nation and language that you impose such harsh decrees against us alone' – and the Romans declared these decrees null and void.
>
> *(Rosh Hashana* 19a)

Influenced perhaps in part by Stoic philosophy, some Jews tried to elevate the virtues of humiliation and the humility of 'those who are insulted and do not insult, who act out of love and find joy in suffering' (*Shabbat* 88b). Phrases such as 'to accept suffering with love' or 'beloved is suffering' have few parallels in pre-70 CE Hebrew literature. They echo Stoic language. According to Joshua ben Levi, true humility was worth all the sacrifices a man could offer in the Temple (*Sotah* 5b) and 'He who accepts sufferings gladly brings salvation to the world' (*Ta'anit* 8a). Akiva, in martyrdom, seeks 'loving acceptance' of divine will:

> When [the Romans] took Akiva out for execution it was time to say the *Shema*. While they raked his flesh with steel combs, he concentrated on the loving acceptance of the yoke of heaven. His pupils said: 'Our rabbi! Even unto this?' He replied: 'All my life I sorrowed over the passage "And you shall love the Lord your God with all your soul" – even if He takes your life. I asked: when will I ever have the chance to fulfil this? Now that I have the chance, should I not fulfil it?' (*Berakhot* 61b)

This need for 'loving acceptance' in the attainment of holiness is echoed by Marcus Aurelius. Despite the differences in nuance between the Hebrew and Greek, the general sense is similar: 'commit the future to providence, and simply seek to direct the present hour aright into the paths of holiness and justice: holiness by a loving acceptance of your appointed lot' (XII 1). Marcus Aurelius' recommendation of wholehearted submission to the divine powers as a means of avoiding subjugation to man is as true of Judaism as of Stoicism. The rabbis taught that man gains freedom through the study of Torah, which reveals to him God's will. According to Joshua ben Levi, 'No man is free unless he studies Torah' (*Avot* 6:2). While the association of Torah study with freedom is uniquely Jewish and has been crucial in the development and survival of Judaism, the idea that a religious philosophy can be liberating is in fact paralleled in the *Meditations*: 'Let the rest of your days be spent as one who has wholeheartedly committed his all to the gods, and is therefore no man's master or slave' (IV 31).

There is some irony – and possibly even hypocrisy – in the ideal of resignation here: Marcus Aurelius spent most of his reign at war; and Akiva, too, according to Jewish tradition, far from accepting the pacifist philosophy of 'loving acceptance', had been a spiritual leader of the Bar-Kokhba revolt. The almost suicidal ferocity of the Jewish revolts itself suggests that such attempts at doormat mentality came in response to defeat, when national pride was at low ebb. At its worst, the stern, self-negating morality of rabbinic Judaism could be stifling in its total submission to the Law. It recalls the Nietzschean view of morality as a revenge on life, even a form of decadence. It is little wonder that modern Zionism, though in some ways deriving nourishment from the nationalist undercurrent of rabbinic Judaism, has been hostile to its passive outlook. The poet W. H. Auden described humiliation as the seedbed of creativity, but the prevailing rabbinic view is expressed in the saying, 'neither suffering nor the reward of suffering' (*Berakhot* 5b).

CONCLUSION

In a possibly apocryphal anecdote set in Israel of the early 1950s, a time of economic depression, one of Ben-Gurion's generals suggested to him that Israel declare war on the United States. Inevitably it would lose and then become the beneficiary of American aid. Ben-Gurion liked this mouse-that-roared idea but was worried about one thing: 'What if we win?'

There was of course no Marshall Plan for Palestine after the failure of the Bar-Kokhba uprising. Yet the Jews took some spiritual and psychological benefits from defeat. Among these was the flourishing of Hebrew literature. Stigmatization of Judaism as deviance in the empire led to the amplification, not erosion, of its distinctive identity.[28] In particular, the loss of a spiritual centre was hardly fatal, though it might have been. What followed was the growth of the synagogue and of rabbinic preaching. This meant better education for the Jewish masses and a wider knowledge of Hebrew; the spread of Jewish schools which cut across class differences; and greater viability of a large Jewish diaspora. The elimination of Temple sacrifice, which was in the long run inevitable and potentially divisive and destructive had the Jews themselves been responsible, was accomplished with brutal neatness by the Romans, who could now be blamed. The rabbis in common with the prophets before them believed that the Jews were punished with exile for their sins. In the view of Rabbi Oshaya, a colleague of Judah Hanasi, this punishment could facilitate Jewish survival: 'God dealt charitably with the Jews by scattering them among the nations' (*Pesahim* 87b).

The destruction of the Temple symbolized the end of the Jews' political and military power. It confined them to more enduring spiritual, cultural and educational concerns. The ruined Temple came to exert a far stronger hold on the Jewish imagination than the Temple when standing. It looms large over Hebrew literature, both halakhic and aggadic. In an acute observation of Rabbi Hiyya bar Ami in the name of the mid 3rd-century rabbi, Ulla, 'From the day the Temple was destroyed, the Holy One, blessed be He, was left with no more than the four cubits of halakhah' (*Berakhot* 8a). Though other Jewish legal codifications were done in the aftermath of disaster and exile – Maimonides' *Mishne Torah* was written after the Almohad invasion of 1140, during which the young Maimonides and his family were exiled from Spain, and Joseph Caro's *Shulḥan Arukh* was written after the Jewish expulsion from Spain in 1492 – the Mishna is the most original and revolutionary of all halakhic literature.

Guided by the Mishna, halakhah as it developed in succeeding centuries was notable for its almost microscopic concern with human matters, for being down to earth and practical: one might almost say that Judaism now bore the imperial stamp. Roman practicality, which is apparent in Hebrew style of the period, was

enhanced by the turn from messianism and mysticism which had
failed to restore Jewish independence in the Bar-Kokhba revolt. In
the absence of an hereditary priesthood, leadership by means of the
mastery of halakhah was open to all. The rabbis set up an intellectual democracy of sorts in which the halakhist was the non-heredi-
tary 'philosopher-king' ruling the less knowledgeable masses. The
clash and resolution of opposing ideas took the place of the clash of
swords in war. And so it remained for two millennia until the 19th
century that leadership in the Jewish world was predominantly
religious, and defined by mastery of halakhah.

Hebrew literature deriving from the period 66–200 CE shows
that the Jews, though defeated and humiliated, were aware that
they had seriously frightened the most powerful empire in
history into turning on them with inordinate force to crush them
militarily and politically. Mendels (1992) points out that 'The Jews
were the only ones who launched a revolution on a grand scale
against Rome in the ancient Near East' (p. 355). Of the initial
success of the Great Revolt in 66 CE, Millar (1993) observes:
'There is no other example of a comparable defeat of Roman
regular forces by the population of an established province' (p.
71). Fear was evident in the extraordinary number of Roman troops
needed to suppress the Jewish uprisings and to keep order between
the revolts and after they ended.[29] Fear also lay behind such
unprecedented actions as the suppression of the Jewish ruling
class, the *fiscus Judaicus*, the destruction of synagogues and the ban
on proselytization. Their wars with Rome ultimately confirmed to
the Jews the futility of military power. They were forced into greater
consciousness of the gap between the necessarily humane values of
halakhic Judaism and those of the empire. Having been conquered,
they turned to virtuous self-conquest in obedience to a legal system
– 'Who is valorous? He who conquers his Evil Inclination' (*Avot* 4:1)
– and to self-consolation in aggadah.

Still, the Jews could hardly have been unaware that their survival
and the growth of Hebrew culture were made possible by the *Pax
Romana*. Vespasian may have defeated them, but he is also credited
with giving them a chance to rebuild their lives on the foundations
of the Torah (*Gittin* 56a–b). The Hebrew literature which they
created might be seen in a broad perspective not as a local, reactive
literature but, together with Roman law and the New Testament, as
an important and enduring legacy of Rome, anticipatory of the
conversion of the empire to monotheism and, later, of the rise of

humanism in the Renaissance. The withdrawal from the empire represented by this literature is also a form of relationship, a cultural bond of unremitting ambivalence.

The new centrality of Jewish education and of Hebrew ensured the survival of Judaism and the Hebrew language and literature and later helped to maintain Jewish distinctiveness and usefulness in European societies which were largely illiterate. The growth of Hebrew in the Mishnaic period thus indirectly had far-reaching consequences not just in the periods to be studied in the next two chapters but also in the development of modern civilization. The effectiveness of Jewish education enabled the Jews ultimately to value and make exceptional use of secular European educational systems when these opened up after the French Revolution. Hebrew literature was temporarily a conduit of this secular education. It may seem strange to think of Marx, Freud, Durkheim, Einstein and Wittgenstein as beneficiaries of Joshua ben Gamla and Rabbi Hiyya. The link is indirect but it is there,

Alive though scarred by the jaws of the Roman lion, the Jews could still look backward with pride and forward with hope. As in the prophetic age, Hebrew gained in prestige by being the language of survival, the chief instrument by which the rabbis ensured the renewal of Jewish life after their defeats by the Romans. The Jews survived with the confidence and optimism of their antiquity; with the belief in being God's chosen people, in Hebrew as the Holy Tongue and in the Hebrew Bible as the word of God; with their anticipation of the coming of the Messiah and of the afterlife; and with their memory of past grandeur, of sovereignty and the Temple. All these sources of pride are expressed memorably in Hebrew literature.

At the same time, the ghettoization of Judaism and the rise of anti-Semitism were foreshadowings of a tragic future. Their acceptance of the hard, unifying yoke of halakhah in some ways cut the Jews off from the non-Jewish world and stifled their artistic powers. For the next two millennia, until the late nineteenth century, there would be frustratingly little of exceptional quality in Hebrew, except for a brief dazzling period in Muslim Spain. For the time being, their unity, though imperfect, represented a victory, if not over the Romans then over themselves, over history and over a God glorying in his own defeat by his beloved children. This, they believed, was the only victory worth having.

3 Hebrew Poetry and the Empire of Islam 1031–1140

From the ruined shell of Rome after the empire's fall, Hebrew literature moved into a new home – the Islamic empire – in the 7th and 8th centuries CE. It is a commonplace that Hebrew poetry reached a 'golden age' – as did Arabic poetry at the same time – in Muslim Spain in the 11th and 12th centuries. Most of this poetry may be dated specifically from the fall of the Umayyad caliphate in 1031 until the Almohad invasion of Spain in 1140. Less common is the observation that this period coincided with, and was inseparable from, a decisive historical shift in the global balance of power. For this was the juncture at which Christian Europe emerged and began to overtake Islam, militarily, economically and culturally. In which ways did the decline of the Islamic empire and the rise of Christian Europe affect Hebrew creativity?

The 11th century was the turning point. By that time, the Islamic empire had split into three caliphates, the Abbasid, Fatimid and Umayyad, the main unifying feature of which was cultural, in particular the use of Arabic. The 11th century began with the collapse of the Umayyad caliphate. It ended with the conquest of Muslim-held Sicily and the east Mediterranean, including Palestine, by the Crusaders. By 1099, Jerusalem was in Christian hands, after four and a half centuries under Islam. The fragmentation of the seemingly stable and powerful Muslim empire in the west Mediterranean into over two dozen city-states (*taifas* = 'parts') led to innumerable civil wars in Spain. Fanatical Berber Muslims invaded from North Africa. Gradually, the Christians reconquered Spain from the north. These upheavals were disastrous for the Jews. Yet, they paradoxically created artificial conditions in which Jewish life in Spain, and Hebrew culture, could temporarily flourish.

This age of imperial collapse and failed recovery in Muslim Spain was marked by two distinct periods: 1. civil war among the splinter-kingdoms; 2. Berber invasions from North Africa. The two Hebrew poets who dominated the first period were Samuel Hanagid (993–1056) and Solomon Ibn Gabirol (1021/2–1056?), of whom Gabirol is acknowledged as the greater. In the second period there were also two outstanding Hebrew poets: Moses Ibn Ezra (*c.*1055–after 1135) and Judah Halevi (*c*.1075–*c*.1141). With Halevi, post-biblical Hebrew poetry reached its artistic peak prior to modern times. The poetry of Hanagid and Gabirol is set against the fall of the Cordoba caliphate, while the poetry of Ibn Ezra and Halevi has for its background the Berber invasions of 1090 and 1140. This explosion of creativity came from a society torn apart by internecine war and the spasmodic drive south by the armies of Christian Spain, yet culturally the most advanced in the Middle Ages.

The poets themselves might have wondered to learn that later generations saw theirs as a golden age. Their own experience was war, chaos, instability and exile, as this brief chronological table shows:

1009–1031	Collapse of the Umayyad caliphate.
1013	Fall of Cordoba. Exile of Samuel Hanagid from Cordoba, his birthplace, to Malaga.
1031–1091	Over two dozen splinter-kingdoms rule Andalusia, often at war with one another.
1066	Massacre of Jewish community of Granada.
1085	Conquest of Toledo by Christian army of Alfonso VI.
1086	Almoravid invasion and defeat of Christian army at al-Zallaqah, near Badajoz.
1090	Destruction of Jewish community of Granada by Almoravids, witnessed by Ibn Ezra and Halevi.
1091–1145	Almoravid rule of Muslim Spain.
1096–1099	First Crusade, culminating in Christian conquest of the Land of Israel from the Muslims.
1135	Capture of Seville by Christian army of Alfonso VII.
1140–1150	Almohad invasion and conquest of Muslim Spain.
1147	Capture of Seville by Almohads. Maimonides and his family, resident in Cordoba, are forced into exile.
1147–1149	Second Crusade

How did Hebrew poetry blossom in such rocky, dangerous soil? From the time of the Arab conquests of the 7th and early 8th centuries until the 13th century, the world Jewish population was still largely concentrated in the Middle East, chiefly in Babylonia under Abbasid rule. Economic decline and political instability, and the shift of the power centre of the Arab world from Baghdad to Cairo in the Fatimid empire, led many Jews to emigrate from Babylonia to North Africa or Spain. Spain, conquered by Muslims in 711, was the frontier not just of Islam but also of the known world. Its large empty spaces and fertile land and its geographical position offered much opportunity within an Arabic culture familiar and congenial to the majority of Jews.

The difficulties endured by the Babylonian Jews, driving them to emigrate, are the subject of an undated liturgical poem by the last great religious leader of Babylonian Jewry, Hai Gaon, who died in 1038 having lived for a century. Hai Gaon gives a bitter account of the precarious state of the Jews who, he writes, have survived countless sorrows only to escape no sorrow before death:[1]

> This the people that never were,
> eaten away, scattered, despoiled.
> Babylonia trounced them, Media knocked them out,
> Greece swallowed them, Islam did not vomit them.
> Why make their yoke heavier?
> Why double their misery?
> Powerless, what can they endure?
>
> *Akhen sar mar ha-mavet* (Carmi, 1981, p. 303)

At the start of the golden age, when these lines were written, most Jews spoke Arabic, which had replaced Aramaic as their *lingua franca*. Jewish immigrants to Spain easily fitted in, especially as the country was a frontier with many new immigrants. The similarities between Islam and Judaism also helped: both are monotheisms which hold that salvation is achieved through obedience to divine commandments as revealed to a supreme prophet; both are based on religious jurisprudence interpreted by scholars and judges; both emphasize the importance of dietary laws and communal worship. Throughout the Arab world, the Jews, like the Christians, had the status of a protected religious group (*dhimma*) and were respected as a 'people of the book' (*ahl al-kitab*), a people who possessed holy scriptures recognized by Islam.

With their ancient, sharply defined religious culture, the Jews went on, in fact, to have a disproportionate influence at a time when Spain, with its highly variegated population, was struggling toward national self-definition. In particular, the Jews' stress on their biblical lineage and chosenness, as well as being the bearers of a divine message in a pure and holy literature, was adopted by Christians and Muslims in shaping Spanish culture. Through its impact upon Europe and its empire overseas, this culture later became a seminal force in the making of modern civilization. Judaism, which was nowhere a state religion (except in the land of the Khazars in the 9th–10th centuries), was the more adaptable under Islamic (and, later, Christian) rule. Psychologically, the Jews' long experience of exile and minority status eased their adaptation to Spanish Muslim society. While the Christians, unused to foreign rule, mostly converted to Islam or fled to Christian Spain, the Jews flourished. Hebrew poetry, their most resplendent cultural monument, is emblematic of the cultural synthesis to which they aspired and, in the end, failed to achieve.

This poetry owes at least some of its exceptional interest to the tension between the drive for acculturation and the inferior position of the Jews in Muslim society. Until modern times, Bernard Lewis has written (1984, p. 102), the Jews under Islamic rule were generally subjected to countless harassments and petty humiliations, to mockery, insult and chronic insecurity; they paid higher taxes than Muslims; they suffered severely restrictive laws of inheritance; they could not carry arms; there were limitations on the animals they could ride, the buildings they could build and the places of worship they could use; they were even limited in the clothes they could wear and were obliged to wear a special emblem, the origin of the notorious yellow star.

In the 10th and 11th centuries, until the Berber invasions, these disabilities were not felt as acutely in Muslim Spain as elsewhere. In fact, there were advantages in being Jewish in Andalusia at this time. Under Abd ar-Rahaman III (912–61), Muslim Spain achieved centralized rule and independence from the Abbasid empire. It quickly became the most powerful, richest and most culturally advanced country in 10th century Europe. Its capital, Cordoba, was one of the largest cities of the time with an estimated quarter of a million inhabitants. Cordoba's central library had some 400,000 volumes (Baron, 1957, IV, p. 28). The Spanish Jews at this time may have numbered no more than 60,000 (Ashtor, 1979, II, p. 34). Yet they were concentrated in the cities, at the hub of the social, economic and political life of Muslim Spain. The creation of an independent caliphate in Spain led to the independence of its Jewish population from Babylonian religious authority, which was in decline.

Consequently, they were readier than in the past to take part in the life of the wider society, to experiment culturally. A sign of this new freedom was their use, for the first time, of secular forms and genres in Hebrew verse.

The manifest superiority of this rich, elegant, cultivated society on Islam's toehold on continental Europe drew settlers from the east. At the start of the golden age, most of the Spanish Christian population were recent converts to Islam (Glick, 1979).[2] The Muslim rulers were a minority among Christians, Jews, neo-Muslims and others and, needing their support, were sharply alive to the importance of tolerance and fairness. To ensure their sense of belonging and their loyalty, the Muslim rulers found it expedient to build a universalist Arab culture, rather than a narrow Islamic religious one. The court was the centre of this culture. The splendid court of Cordoba and, later, the courts of the splinter kingdoms, created opportunities for Jewish courtiers. Imitating their Arab colleagues, they became patrons of Hebrew poets. The importance of courts and of patronage in the golden age may be seen in the fact that when the courts vanished and patronage ceased, Hebrew and Arabic poetry declined. The Jews' alliance with Islamic sovereignty and the concomitant golden age of Hebrew poetry is best understood in the context of the ethnic and religious diversity and conflicts of Hispano-Arab society and its socio-religious problems (Wasserstein, 1985; Brann, 1991).[3]

The Jews, furthermore, comprised an essential part of the middle class. There was hardly a profession in which Jews were not active. Because of their considerable trading links, their cosmopolitanism and knowledge of languages, the Jews were invaluable as translators, courtiers and diplomats. Their talents were also a rich source of revenue. The shift of power in Andalusia in the 10th century from the aristocratic elite to the middle class worked to the Jews' advantage, especially in cities such as Granada, where they formed a large part of the population. Hebrew creativity expressed Jewish pride and self-confidence stemming from social and economic success and political power. A point alluded to earlier should be stressed: Spain's geographic position on the frontier of Christian Europe bordering the great unexplored Atlantic helped break down social barriers between Muslims and Jews. The cooperation and social harmony between them were virtually unique in the Middle Ages and unrepeated in modern times.

THE CULTURAL BACKGROUND OF THE GOLDEN AGE

How did these social conditions make Hebrew poetry blossom, and what role did this verse play in the lives of the Spanish Jews? Medieval Hebrew poetry had a long, complex socio-linguistic germination. A number of factors in addition to those given above were of special importance in promoting literature, stimulating cultural imitation and competition, and in heightening sensitivity to the Hebrew language and sharpening its usage:

1. Christian biblical exegetes often undermined Jewish interpretation. They forced Jewish exegetes, many of whom wrote Hebrew poetry, to study closely the vocabulary and grammar of the Bible in order to refute the Christians and achieve a clear interpretation of the Hebrew text.

2. The Karaites, a fundamentalist Jewish sect, denied the sacred character of the Oral Law and of post-biblical Hebrew. They insisted instead that authentic Judaism was confined to the literal truth of the Five Books of Moses. The dispute with the Karaites, who had considerable influence in the 9th and 10th centuries and after, had the effect of forcing their 'Rabbanite' opponents to stop their neglect of the Bible and achieve greater awareness of the nuances of the Hebrew text.

3. The proliferation since the late-Roman period of synagogues led to an increasing demand for original Hebrew liturgical poetry which entered the Hebrew prayer book (*Siddur*). The earliest prayer books were edited in the 8th or 9th centuries (Reif, 1993). All the great medieval Hebrew poets wrote for the synagogue as well as for secular reading.

4. The golden age was part of a general flourishing of Jewish literature – legal, homiletical, polemical, exegetical, philological, as well as liturgical – in the years 900–1200 (Baron, 1958, VII, p. 136). This literature was facilitated by the reunification of the majority of the world's Jewish population under Islamic rule and by the intellectual stimulus of the rise of Islam. It was also part of a great surge in European literary activity resulting from a revolution in book manufacturing. Paper reached the Islamic empire by the end of the 8th century. Within two centuries, Spain became a world centre of paper manufacture and the production of books.

5. The increasing split between Jews living under Muslim and Christian rule made vital the use of Hebrew in contacts between the two groups.

6. The explosion in the use of Arabic and the growth of Islamic court culture in which Arabic was used in the 8th and 9th centuries led to an enrichment of the Arabic language and a high valuation of correct grammar, stylistic excellence and beautiful calligraphy:

> Perhaps in no period in human history did preoccupation with the correctness and purity of the spoken and written language become such a deep concern of the educated classes as during the Islamic Renaissance.
>
> (Baron, 1958, VII, p. 3)

The divine inspiration and truth of the Koran were believed by the Arabs to be proven by its stylistic excellence; the Jews adopted a similar belief about the Hebrew Bible. As the first fully bilingual group of Jewish writers, the Hebrew poets of Muslim Spain were well-acquainted with Arabic and the Koran, though as infidels they were discouraged from writing Arabic. In any case, they were convinced that Hebrew was superior to all languages: it was more ancient and beautiful and, above all, the language in which God had revealed himself in the Bible. They revolted against the eastern style of Hebrew poetry associated with Saadia Gaon, with its over-abundant, enigmatic talmudic and midrashic allusions. Instead, they favoured clear biblical language. Their poetry was further influenced by the rediscovery of ancient Greek learning, with its emphasis on philosophy and rhetoric. This resurrection led to a marked increase in the vocabulary and intellectual depth of Arabic language and thought, which Hebrew writers adopted in Hebrew.

POETRY, THE COURT AND ISLAM

The pre-eminent importance attached to poetry in the Islamic empire was the single main catalyst for Hebrew poetry, which was enriched immeasurably in imitation of and competition with Arabic poetry. This influence was not mutual, however: non-Jewish Arabic readers did not usually read Hebrew, and Hebrew poetry was apparently not translated into Arabic. Still the high status of Hebrew poetry among the Spanish Jews at this time was probably unique in Jewish history. Whole cities, such as Lucena and Seville, were known as 'cities of poetry'. Court life brought into being the professional Hebrew poet, employed by Jewish courtiers such as the physician and statesman Hasdai Ibn Shaprut (*c.* 905–*c.* 970), whose prominent position in the court of the above-mentioned Abd ar-Rahaman III made him the natural leader of the Jews in Muslim Spain. Imitating his Arab colleagues, Ibn Shaprut became the patron of scholars and poets. These included the two Hebrew poets who created the artistic basis for the golden age: Menahem Ibn Saruq (*c.* 910–*c.* 970) and Dunash ben Labrat (?–*c.*970). Neither had outstanding poetic gifts. Yet, ben Labrat revolutionized Hebrew poetry by imitating the quantitative metres and secular themes of Arabic poetry. He was also the first to criticize the artificiality of forcing Hebrew verse into Arabic prosody and the blasphemy of using the Holy Tongue for secular purposes. This criticism reached its bitterest expression in the writings of Judah Halevi. The golden age ironically began and ended with blasts at its own art. However, the criticism of Hebrew poetry was also imitative: the Arabs, too, frequently voiced similar complaints against Arabic poetry of the Cordoba caliphate. This poetry was often felt to reflect the artificiality and corruption of court life, the abuse of artists as functionaries flattering their patrons, sycophantically toeing the party line.

Both Hebrew and Arabic poetry were galvanized by the fall of the caliphate and the rise of the splinter kingdoms in the first half of the 11th century. The technical and thematic revolution of the 10th century was now harnessed to a radical change in psychological outlook and sensibility. For a brief period, both literatures created poetry of exceptional artistic quality, if not genius.

The Jews had mastered the dominant high culture of the early Middle Ages and gained entrée into the highest social and political circles at the zenith of the Umayyad caliphate. Now they realized that their position under Muslim rule in Spain was untenable. Precisely at this moment – in the first half of the 11th century – the Jews reached the high point of their political power and cultural achievement between the destruction of the Second Temple and modern times. Why was this so? One explanation is that the Jews, as part of a society in chaos, were liberated for a while from the normal social shackles of being Jewish in the medieval world. The Hebrew poet was, to an extent, temporarily free of social constraint and able to use advances in Hebrew poetry to find an original poetic voice. Like Van Gogh's sunflowers, this golden Hebrew culture was dying, and dying in the very poetry which was its brightest sign of life.

The destruction of court society centralized in Cordoba meant the end of 'official' court poetry. It freed the individual poet, Muslim and Jew, to explore personal emotion as a subject worthy of poetry (Monroe, 1975, p. 21). The social anarchy described in the poetry of Hanagid and Gabirol belongs specifically to the 11th century. The following lines by Gabirol, though typically they echo a biblical passage (Micah 7:6), could not describe 10th-century Andalusia, when the caliphate was strong. They are a grim picture of the chaos, civil strife and despair which prevailed in Andalusia after the caliphate fell apart:

> Man has no joy on earth:
> Slave murders master.
> Servant girls attack their queen.
> Son strikes parents.
> Daughter does the same.
> Friend, the best remedy I know – madness.

> *Ve-lev navuv*

The social stratification in Muslim Spain, already greatly weakened in the course of the 10th century, was largely swept aside. The splinter kingdoms, battling among themselves, sought allies – Jews and Christians alike – where they could find them. As a result, Jews were allowed to take part in Islamic society to a degree unprecedented in Islamic history and unrepeated since.

In this chaotic state of transition, Arabic poets such as Ibn Hazm (994–1064) and Ibn Zaidun (1003–1071) and their contemporary Hebrew poets Hanagid and Gabirol, created a body of poetry extraordinary in its emphasis upon the individual sensibility as well as its technical mastery. The following lines by Ibn Hazm, for example, strike a new note in Arabic poetry:

> I am seen as a youth desperate with love,
> my heart broken, my spirit troubled. By whom?
> Men discern my state and are sure,
> but on closer scrutiny are left in doubt.
> I am like clear handwriting, meaning obscure,
> like a dove cooing every which way
> in its little forest, delighting the ear
> with its melody, its meaning untapped . . .

A girl once loved me, I surprised her with a kiss:
That kiss was my only life, however long my life is.

(Monroe, 1975, pp. 174–5)[4]

The poetry of Ibn Zaidun, likewise, is animated by a rare sense of real emotion and people. Most of Ibn Zaidun's poems were inspired by his love for an Umayyad princess in the last days of the caliphate and for some time after. His poems of lost love recreate a world that has vanished but are at the same time deeply personal:

Yes, I remembered you, longed for you, as you were
in az-Zahara', the sky blue, earth alight,
the evening breeze languid with pity for me.
And the garden smiled. A day like the lost pleasure time
we thieved our nights away as fortune slept.
Flowers caught our eye, bent with dew as if in tears
for my sleeplessness.

(Arberry, 1965, pp. 114–15)

In the poetry of Ibn Zaidun, Arabic poetry reached an artistic peak, described by Albert Hourani as 'the last flowering of an original and personal lyrical [Arabic] poetry before modern times' (1990, p. 194).[5] The same is true of Ibn Zaidun's Hebrew contemporaries, whose best work is unequalled until modern times.

HANAGID AND GABIROL

The new individual tone of Arabic poetry reached Hebrew with lasting impact in the poetry of Hanagid. Hanagid had an exceptionally varied and interesting life and career, though what is known of his life can be summed up in a few lines. As well as being the first major Hebrew poet of the golden age, he was also an important rabbi, leader of the Granada Jewish community, ultimately first citizen of Granada as vizier (from 1027) and minister of war (from 1038), commander of the Berber Muslim army for nearly two decades of almost constant war. He reportedly never lost a battle.

The complexity of Hanagid's career and the extent of his power are themselves clear signs of the new life chances which opened to Jews in Muslim Spain after the fall of the caliphate. The formative trauma of Hanagid's early manhood was, in fact, the the end of the caliphate – the horrific siege of Cordoba, his hometown, by the Berbers. This siege lasted for several years until the Umayyad capital fell in 1013. Exiled from his native city, Hanagid was an eyewitness of the appalling effects of the fall of the caliphate and the civil wars which followed. His rise to power in Granada was, paradoxically, made possible by the very fact of his being Jewish. The Jews, representing the economic strength of the middle class, helped create a precarious stability in the balance of power between the Berber rulers and the Arab aristocratic elite. Hanagid also saw how the neighbouring Christian powers began what amounted to a protection racket by which the fragile Muslim kingdoms obtained military aid against their Muslim rivals. He cursed the Christians in impeccable metre and rhyme and called for the renewal of his people:

> Evil queen, cease your reign!
> Reign instead, hated Jews,
> long asleep on bed of pain.
> Wake! There's medicine for you,
> and recompense for being true.

> *Malkah resha'ah*[6]

The fascination of Hanagid lies in the contradictions of general and poet, leader of an Arab army and head of the Granada Jewish community, public man and tough individualist, religious Jew and secular poet. The toughness and directness of some of his war poetry had not appeared in Hebrew since the Bible and were not to appear again until the 20th century, when most Hebrew poets have also been soldiers:

> I stationed a regiment in a fortress
> destroyed long ago in war.
> There we slept, below us the dead...
> If they woke to life, they'd kill us
> and take everything we have.
> It's God's own truth, by tomorrow
> we'd all be stone-cold as they.

> *Halinoti gedud*

The kingdom of Seville was Granada's main rival. Many of Hanagid's poems describe wars which he fought against Seville.

Although Hanagid commanded a Muslim army, he writes as though Jews are at war with the infidel, not Muslims fighting Muslims. (He never mentions that there were Jews in the armies against which he fought.) Instead, his victories are the victories of the Jewish God:

> In Seville they did evil to the Jews –
> conspiracy, weapons, chains –
> to murder Jewish mothers and babies,
> rich and poor alike.
>
> We laughed when their king spoke arrogantly.
> We crossed the border to avenge our people,
> our warriors savage as lions,
> we swarmed in on them like locusts...
>
> God tied their hands with rope,
> their hearts too.
> They stumbled over their chariots,
> their horses chains on their feet.
>
> In a word, he broke them
> as a weaver snaps thread.
> Famous warriors in chains,
> dragged before the king –
> at his will they lived or died.
>
> I was faint at the bloody torture,
> the pampered foot stabbed with thorns,
> warriors' corpses tossed on a pile.
>
> *Ha-li ta'as bekhol shanah*[7]

The Arabs led by Hanagid were not so secular as to overcome their prejudice against him as an infidel Jew, damned to perdition; neither were they so devout as to shirk from the leadership of an inordinately gifted Jew. As a prominent figure in the Granada court, Hanagid had his Jewish retinue, including the young Gabirol who seems to have admired Hanagid's poetry as well as his statesmanship. In one of his panegyrics for Hanagid, Gabirol compares him with his namesake, the prophet Samuel:

> Wisdom-seeker, delver into her mysteries
> to gather her from exile,

> making her treasures his,
> her silver and gold.

Mi zot ke-mo shahar

To Gabirol, Hanagid was a model of the synthesis to which he aspired between Arab culture and Jewish tradition. As a poet, however, Gabirol went much further than Hanagid in using the new-found freedom of Andalusian poetry. Whereas much of Hanagid's poetry is outgoing and public, Gabirol's is deeply personal. The sadness and loneliness in Gabirol's poetry is unparalleled in any other medieval Hebrew poet. His works describe his physical and mental torture. He knew that the hoped-for cultural synthesis between Jews and Muslims in Spain was a pipe-dream:

> I am buried – not in a desert but in my house,
> my coffin. I agonize, orphaned of mother and father,
> brotherless. Young, alone, poor. Thought
> is my only friend. My tears are stirred in blood and wine,
> thirsting for a friend –
> I will die before that thirst is quenched.
> The heavens block my yearning.
> Alien am I to all.

Nihar be-kor'i groni

> If you want to join the man forever young,
> as your soul gutters by the underworld's flame –
> mock worldly things, be not the fool
> of wealth and honour, a son to have your name.
>
> Value poverty and humility, then die
> as Seled did, with no son.
> Try to know your soul well. It alone
> will live when skin and flesh are gone.

Im te'ehav lihyot be-anshe Heled[8]

The execution of Gabirol's patron, Yekutiel ben Isaac ibn Hassan, in 1039 confirmed his apprehensions about the future. It is recorded in the following lyric:[9]

> See the sun red-cloaked at dusk,
> stripping itself of north and south,
> dressing itself crimson,

leaving the land naked, to sleep
in night's dark shelter.
Then the sky went black as a sack
for the death of Yekutiel.

Re'eh shemesh

In the face of outrage to his body, his soul and his social world,
Gabirol retreats to his infinitely gentle, suffering spirit, to a dialogue
with soul or Creator. The poet is trapped in a shifting no-man's-
land in the long religious war between Muslims and Christians, in
which the Jews are losers. Terrified, he calls to God, the beloved in
rabbinic interpretations of the Song of Songs:[10]

Open the gate, my love!
Get up, open the gate!
I tremble in terror. Mother's slave,
Hagar, mocked me in her arrogance,
for God heard her son Ishmael's cry.
In the dead of night
the wild-ass Muslims chased me,
the wild-boar Christians trampled me.
When my exile's end was fixed
my heartache grew worse.
No one can explain – and I am dumb.

Sha'ar petaḥ

SOCIAL BREAKDOWN IN ANDALUSIA AND HEBREW CREATIVITY

The pessimism of Gabirol's poetry foreshadowed the end of
Andalusian Jews under Muslim rule. In 1066, Hanagid's son,
Joseph, who had succeeded him as vizier of Granada, was murdered. In one of the earliest pogroms in European history, about
3,000 Jews of Granada were massacred. An Arabic poem by Abu
Ishaq helped trigger off the pogrom. It incited Badis ibn Habbus,
king of Granada, to wipe out Jewish influence in the Granada
government:

This was Badis' fatal mistake, making our enemy rejoice:
Not Muslim but Jew he made his minister.

> Now the Jews are not just low-down:
> They're arrogant, insolent too.
> They got more than they ever dreamed of,
> ignoring Muslims dying in misery.
> How many noble Muslims are brought low
> before this wretched monkey-Jew!

(Monroe, 1975, pp. 206–7)

This poem, and the violence which followed, was the turning point in the history of the Andalusian Jews. Ashtor (1979) describes this pogrom as a clear warning that they were living on an erupting volcano:

> The slaughter in Granada showed them the tenuousness of their position in alien lands. Over the generations they had come to believe that they were as much citizens of Spain as were the Muslims and Christians, the Andalusians and Arabs, the Berbers and Slavs – now it was clear: Spain was a land of exile as were all the other diasporas.

(II, p. 191)

As in Russia 700 years later, anti-Jewish violence in Muslim Spain was a gauge of general political and social instability, not just in the splinter kingdoms that had inherited the Umayyad empire but in the Islamic world as a whole, as the balance of power between Muslims and Christians shifted to the clear advantage of the Christians. The lack of strong central authority in the Arab empire led to political breakdown and to Christian military success, in Spain and the Holy Land. The Christians won control of trade in the Mediterranean. The Muslims lost economic power in lands controlled by Islam. The defeats in Spain and the Holy Land at the end of the 11th century were not just military blows. They were also unprecedented religious and psychological setbacks to Islam. They led to growing fanaticism among the Muslims, which increasingly soured relations between Muslims and Jews. To devout Muslims, the integration of Jews within Spanish Muslim society was a sign of defeat, even of moral decline and corruption. After the fall of Toledo in 1085, the splinter kingdoms invited the Almoravid Berbers to cross the Strait of Gibraltar to save them from the Christian infidel. In 1086 the Berbers defeated the Christian army of Alfonso VI of Castile at Sagrajas. Between 1090–1102 they ended the disunity which had prevailed since 1031. They seized Andalusia and made it a province of their North African empire. This military feat led to the migration of most Andalusian Jews to Christian Spain. Unexpectedly, it heralded an Indian summer of Hebrew poetry.

IBN EZRA AND JUDAH HALEVI

Hanagid and Gabirol were wholly Andalusian poets in the time of the splinter kingdoms and civil wars. Ibn Ezra and Halevi were born in Andalusia but after the Almoravid invasion were exiled to Christian Spain. Despite maltreatment by the Andalusian Muslims, Ibn Ezra remained nostalgic for the Andalusia of his youth. No other Hebrew poet applied so expertly Arabic metrics, themes and images to Hebrew.[11] The following poem, for example, bears an Arabic imprint in its metre (in the Hebrew: ABCBDB), its imagery and feeling:

> Let man always know
> unto death he moves.
> As day to night creeps past
> he may think he is at rest –
> at rest on a boat
> flying in the wind.
>
> *Yizkor gever*

Ibn Ezra's affection for Andalusia evidently grew as he discovered the pains of being a stranger and a Jew in Christian Spain. In one of his poems, *Pnei ha-El levad*, the world is a mother with a stillborn child in her belly and a dying child on her back. He might have been thinking of his own life. To Ibn Ezra as to Gabirol, poetry consoled the poet and his readers:

> You who are heartsick and cry bitterly –
>   do not grieve.
> Come into the garden of my poems
>   to find medicine, sung aloud.
> Compared to them honey is bitter
>   incense stinks: these poems make the deaf hear
> the stammerer speak, the blind see,
>   the lame run. The grieving, the heartsick,
> those who cry bitterly find joy in them.
>
> *Kol ish deveh levav*

In poems written to Halevi, his protégé, he poured out his heart:

> Even my enemies
> take pity, while my obstinate brother refuses
> to admit his folly has stripped me
> of everything precious. My children
> too betray me; strangers hurry to dress
> the wound my flesh and blood inflicted.
> Will I ever again find the strength
> to take up the wanderer's staff fate
> thrust into my hands? Mornings I chew
> twigs for my hunger, at dusk
> stagnant water quenches my thirst.
> I sink deeper and deeper
> into a pit of depression, and barely
> pull myself out. My eyes are glazed
> with wandering, my innards
> rumble like the sea, my nerves are on edge.
> I dwell among wolves for whom
> the word human means nothing.

> (Levin, 1992, pp. 35–6)

Halevi, whose own unhappiness led him to a fervent nationalist longing to return to Zion, vainly entreated Ibn Ezra in verse to return to his native land:

> How can I find peace with you gone?
> My heart beats after you.
> If I left off waiting for your return
> I'd die. Look, the mountains of our separation
> testify: clouds are cheap with rain. I cry buckets.
> Come back to Muslim Spain, lamp of Muslim Spain.
> Make your mark on every heart and hand.
> Pure of speech among the stammerers:
> Why spread Hermon's dew on cursed Gilead?

> *Ekh aharecha emtza margo'a*

Halevi was born in Tudela, then under Muslim rule, near the Christian border. As a young man, he came south to Granada where he met Ibn Ezra. The Almoravid invasion drove him to Toledo, only recently captured by the Christians, where he worked as a doctor. After the Toledo Jews were set on by a bloodthirsty mob in 1109 and his patron was murdered, Halevi came back to Andalusia. He lived in Cordoba for some thirty years. When the Almohads invaded southern Spain in 1140, he set out for the Holy Land. It is not known if he reached his destination.

The two decisive events in Halevi's life were the Almoravid invasion and the Christian conquest of the Holy Land. The first aroused his disillusionment with Muslim Spain – indeed, with any form of gentile rule – and the second his yearning for messianic redemption and the return to the Land of Israel. To the North African scholar, Rabbi Habib, Halevi confessed in a letter that 'Greece and its wisdom have drowned me in thick black grease; Islam and Arabic have blackened me; Christianity has torn me apart, destroyed me' (Brann, 1991, p. 90). In poetic dialogues between the Congregation of Israel and God (the Lover), again based on the Midrash on the Song of Songs, Halevi conveys the torment of being trapped between two rival religions:

> Friend – suffering forces me to live
> with viper and scorpion, captive.
> Pity me!
>
> I despair of sunrise.
> Day by day I cannot hope.
>
> What can I say, lover?
>
> Crusaders, freeborn, in Jerusalem, my palace,
> while I slave for Arab and Christian –
> a dog in their tormenting hands.

> *Yodi, hefitzuni yeme oni*

Lover, have you forgot how you lay between my breasts?
Why have you sold me for all time?
Did I not follow you in the wilderness?
Let the mountains be my witnesses –
Seir and Paran, Sinai and Sin!
My love was yours, you wanted just me –
how can you share yourself with others?
I am crushed by the Persians,
scorched by the Greeks,
thrust among Christians, driven among Muslims:
Is there a saviour but you?

A prisoner of hope but me?
Give me your power, I'll give you my love!

Yedidi, hashakhaḥta

The suffering of the people of Israel is seen by the poet as punishment and expiation for sin. Israel takes almost masochistic pleasure in its persecution – this is God's will, but it is also God's will to free his people as he did in the past:

Since you became love's home,
my loves are pitched by you.
My enemies' curse makes me glad.
Let them curse me – as you did.
They learned to hate from you
and I love them – they hound the one you hurt.
The day you scorned me I felt the same.
How can I love the one you hate?
Till your fury goes and you free again
your people whom you freed from Egypt.

Me'az me'on ahavah

The conquest of the Holy Land by the Crusaders after four and a half centuries of Muslim rule was a disaster to the Jewish communities of Palestine (as of those in Europe). Yet it also awakened the Jewish hope of return to the Land of Israel at a time when the majority of the world's Jewish population was still in the Middle East. The memory of Hanagid's military triumphs was still green: if Jerusalem could be captured by Christians, could it not someday fall to the Jews?

A further stimulus in Halevi's poetry was the rise of the Almohads in the second and third decades of the 12th century. The Almohads, as mentioned previously, were a fanatical North African Berber tribe. Unlike the Almoravids, they were also a messianic movement whose founder was believed to be the messiah, destined to restore Islam to the true path and create a kingdom of heaven on earth. The Almohads were, in fact, the last gasp of the Islamic empire which had ruled Andalusia since 711. They ended Andalusian Jewish life under Islam when they invaded in 1140, but they might also have stirred up parallel Jewish messianic hopes, such as those expressed in Halevi's writings. Such hopes are often a sign of social trouble. Halevi's decision to go to the Holy Land, to which his poetry points as inevitable, may be seen as part of a more general religious upheaval involving Muslims and Christians as well as Jews.

Halevi's poems of longing for Zion are among the best-known Hebrew poems outside the Bible. Yet they belong to no genre or tradition. Rather, they are the response of one unusually gifted poet to a decisive crisis in medieval Jewish life. They express nostalgia not just for a Zion that Halevi had never seen – and which had never existed except in the world of Jewish legend – but also, implicitly, for a lost, once powerful and splendid Andalusia in which great hopes and illusions had died.[12] In these poems, a western voice speaks at a time when the demographic process that was to bring most Jews westward was not yet completed. For brief moments, Hebrew, engaging the obsession closest to its heart, breaks out of the shackles of Arabic ornamentation and speaks with real individuality and passion:

> My heart is in the east and I –
> on the end of the west: how can I enjoy,
> how taste my food, how keep my vows
> while Zion is in Christian hands
> and I in Arab chains.
> I'd lightly leave the good of Spain
> to see the Temple's dust again.
>
> *Libi be-mizraḥ*

> Zion, will you not ask about your captives?
> They ask for you, the last of your flock.
> Accept their greeting, west and east, north and south,
> far and near on every side; my greeting too,
> lust-locked to weep Hermon's dew across your hills:
> A jackal I am, wailing out your grief,
> a harp for the dream-song of your exiles' homecoming.
>
> *Zion, ha-lo tishali*

The longing and searching of the Zion poems were not literary conventions. They were true feelings of the poet, driving him in his old age to leave Spain for Palestine. The plangent, questing mood of the Zion poems pervades Halevi's work, the secular love poems as well as the liturgical ones.

> Ofra washes her clothes in my tears.
> She spreads them in the sunshine of her life.

She has no need of fountains,
nor sun to beautify her light.

Ofra tekhabes

Time's slaves – slaves of slaves,
but God's servant is free.
For his part in life man prays:
My part in you I see.

Avdei zeman

God, where can I find you,
hidden in heaven on high?
And where can I not find you –
you fill the universe with glory!

Yah, ana emtza'akha

CONCLUSION: HEBREW POETRY AND ISLAMIC SOCIETY

With Halevi's departure forever from Spain in 1140 – he died a year or two later – and the Almohad conquest of Andalusia, the Jews of Muslim Spain and Hebrew poetry were exiled. By the start of the 13th century, the Almohads were themselves defeated by Christian armies. The empire of Islam was squeezed out of Europe. The flowering of Hebrew poetry in the years 1031–1140 was the final creation of a dying empire that had made Spain the cultural centre of the Western world. It was a long goodbye of a minority once integrally a part of this empire, whose alienation and demise marked the empire's fall.

Each of the major poets of the golden age brought a revolutionary new quality to Hebrew: the confident, aggressive voice of Hanagid; psychological anguish bound up with a philosophical system in Gabirol; the dedication to poetry as a world in its own right, for its own sake, in Ibn Ezra; romantic longing for a distant time and a faraway land in Halevi. Yet, few if any poems of this period are incontestable works of genius. To unsympathetic readers, Hanagid is emotionally shallow and repetitive, Gabirol melancholy and obscure, Ibn Ezra unoriginal, Halevi sentimental. Hebrew poets forced on themselves a crippling prosody: Arabic metrics and techniques, rhetoric and thematic conventions. The creation of standard Arabic and the establishment of clear readings of the Koran for a diverse and growing Muslim population had affected the Arabic language adversely:

> When the philologists received wide-spread recognition from the upper strata of society it was difficult for the would-be poet not to adhere to the canons of language and style they established. This led to artificiality, with the emphasis on the manner of saying a thing rather than on the meaningful content.
>
> (Watt, 1984, p. 48)

In the past, Hebrew poetry had never served merely as ornamental prose, as in Arabic. It was, after all, the language in which God had created the universe, in which he had given the Ten Commandments at Sinai. Now, cliché-ridden and prettily artificial, it was largely sapped of its power, its natural beauty and emotional depth. The overwhelming influence of the Bible was also detrimental, leading to slavish adherence to biblical language and imagery – partly in imitation of Arabic poetry's emulation of the Koran, partly because the brilliance of the Bible overshadowed medieval Hebrew – and a perverse, illusory ideal of biblical 'purity' of language. Detachment from living, spoken Hebrew also contributed to the excessively literary approach to poetry, which was to pervade Hebrew literature until the time of Bialik, in which clever linguistic pyrotechnics were more highly valued than clear, direct speech. As shown previously, some Hebrew poets, notably Halevi, actually confessed their bitter awareness that they had worked their way into an artistic straitjacket.[13]

Why, then, did they write Hebrew poetry in this form? Their works on philosophy and linguistics – for example, Hanagid's *Sefer ha-Osher*, Gabirol's *Mekor Ḥayim*, Ibn Ezra's *Sefer Shirat Yisrael*, and Halevi's *Kuzari* were all written in Arabic. Why not Hebrew poetry as well? To attempt to answer this question is, in effect, to probe the nature of Jewish acculturation within the empire of Islam.

The golden age was both powered and undermined by a conflict of loyalties. The most revolutionary aspect of medieval Hebrew literature was its secular content. Hebrew for the first time became a vehicle for a lifestyle alien to traditional Judaism. Inasmuch as it was influenced by the Andalusian Arab aristocracy, with their love of beauty and pursuit of fleeting pleasure, this poetry betrayed the religious ideals of Judaism, its stress on self-discipline, divine judgement and life in the hereafter. Yet none of the Hebrew poets abandoned traditional Jewish faith and practice. To the contrary, unlike their Arabic contemporaries, the Hebrew poets were often rabbis, religious judges, scholars and biblical exegetes, or a combination of these. (Isaac Ibn Ghiyyat, the innovative 11th-century *paytan*, was head of a yeshiva in Lucena.) They kept Muslim society at arm's length in a number of ways: by writing in a language which Arabs generally did not know; by expressing in these writings a stern loyalty to Judaism and a conviction of the inferiority of other religions, including Islam; by championing the Hebrew Bible as the model of stylistic excellence; and by making a vast contribution to synagogue liturgy. (Though their liturgical poetry inevitably drew on identical vocabulary, idiom, themes and grammatical contructions as their secular poetry, it did not adhere strictly to the metrical forms and rhyme schemes of secular verse.)

Their poetry certainly suggests at times all sorts of behaviour not normally associated with rabbis. Imagine an important contemporary orthodox rabbi found to have written the following lines:

> Plunge into pleasure, have a good time!
> Raise the flask, down the wine!
> Dance ecstatic to birdsong and lyre!
> Clap hands, drunk by the riverside!
> Bang at the door of that good-looking girl!

Dadei yefat to'ar

The author of these lines, Moses Ibn Ezra, understandably came to be embarrassed by such poetry especially as in his later years he was famous for his penitential poems (*selihot*) – so much so that he was known as *ha-salah* (the penitential poet). Still, his secular poetry is typical of Arabic poetry in Andalusia which can be read to express nothing more than wine-song conventions. Such poetry is no hard evidence that medieval Hebrew poets were sexually licentious or engaged in any form of social impropriety. In fact, these poets often expressed severe guilt at the very act of creating secular poetry. Only Hanagid seems to have been free of such guilt.

Aimed though it was exclusively at Jews, medieval Hebrew poetry attempted cultural synthesis, alliance and mimicry, assimilation and competition. The enthusiasm for this assimilation ideal was such that it might have led some Hebrew poets to adopt at times a secular voice alien to them. In any case, their hope for assimilation was overly optimistic, even illusory. Symptomatic of the twisted state of Jewish–Muslim relations of the latter part of the 'golden age' is the fact that the most famous Jewish philosophical work of this period, Halevi's *Kuzari*, written in Arabic, was a defence of the allegedly inferior religion, Judaism. More than this, '*The Kuzari* was a glorification of rabbinic Judaism and an unabashed statement of nationalism in the modern sense of the word' (Stillman, 1979, p. 60). Such a work would, of course, have been unlikely if the Jews had been accepted as equals in Arab society. Especially after the pogrom in Granada in 1066, it was clear that the Jews were not tolerated in positions of power under Muslim rule.

The artificiality of Hebrew poetry might be seen in this light as an inadvertent enactment of the artificiality and awkwardness of Jewish life under Muslim rule in medieval Spain.

In this Hebrew poetry, bitter despondency toward Arab society was implicitly far greater than that toward any aspect of Judaism. Jewish acculturation in Muslim Spain was based on the assumption of a realizable parity within a tolerant, essentially secular Arabic civilization. The fall of the Umayyad empire led, instead, to a failure of Arab universalism and a resurgence of Islamic religious militancy in which the Jews were seen as part of the problem of the empire's decline. The nationalist undercurrent in Hebrew poetry may be seen as a reaction to this exclusivist zealotry.

In the *Kuzari*, Halevi argues that the Jews are distinguished above all other peoples through their capacity to receive divine prophecy. Only in the Land of Israel could they fulfil their prophetic destiny. Such views are not found among the earlier poets of the golden age, such as Hanagid and Gabirol. They betray the poet's disillusionment with Muslim Spain. The strongest thrust of Hebrew poetry in the years immediately prior to the Almohad invasion was a nagging unease and, at times, despair with the host country. Consequently, Hebrew poets created an ideal alternative world in their poetry.

Arabic metres and thematic formulations continued for many generations after the end of Jewish life in Muslim Spain. This influence was a conscious acknowledgement of the artistic possibilities of these poetics. It was also willy-nilly a nostalgic bow to the past, an adios to what might have been, to a marriage of two cultures which failed. This was an irony of the Jewish exile. The most successful Jewish acculturation within a dominant empire between the destruction of the Second Temple and modern times occurred in the tiny province of Andalusia in the 11th century, riven by civil war, by the threat of Christian crusade and Islamic fundamentalism. Here Hebrew poetry blazed like a sun in its final light. As the Assyrians did not know of the Bible and the Romans knew nothing of the Talmud, so also the Arabs remained ignorant of the great cultural efflorescence to which they gave birth and death.

4 Hebrew in the Tsarist Empire 1881–1917

The renascence of the Hebrew language and literature in Tsarist Russia between the outbreak of the progroms in 1881 and the 1917 revolution is arguably the most important development in Hebrew since the Bible. Hebrew literature was the main cultural spur to the rise of modern Jewish nationalism. The Russian Jewish population prior to 1881 had been moving toward increased acculturation within the Tsarist empire and had hopes of emancipation and civil rights. They were deeply wounded, psychologically as well as economically, by Russian government policies legislated in a futile reactionary struggle to adapt to major changes in socioeconomic conditions and the international balance of power.

In common with other creative groups of Hebrew artists prior to 1948 – the prophets, the *tannaim*, the poets of the 'golden age' in medieval Muslim Spain – artistic breakthrough in 1881–1917 may be shown to coincide and to be connected with crisis in the dominant empire. The literature of 1881–1917 continued the pattern of these earlier periods. Crisis in the Tsarist empire led to heightened Jewish national identity. As in the earlier periods, this literature is, among other things, a record of imperial upheaval, social and cultural metamorphosis and wanton violence. The very fact of writing Hebrew itself expressed, or implied, a strong current of religious-nationalist feeling. The main difference between Hebrew literature in the Tsarist empire and its antecedents is its predominantly secular character.

This chapter sets out the historical and literary background to Hebrew literature of 1881–1917, describes some of its salient qualities and influences, particularly in Russian literature, and interprets the reasons for its artistic distinctiveness. It will be argued that Hebrew literature, in common with contemporary Russian literature of the pre-1881 era, might be interpreted *ipso facto* as an act of subversion. It represents on one level a rejection of Tsarist authority, an assertion of Jewish national feeling and a declaration of independence from the empire. In doing so, it engaged in a dynamic relationship with the dominant literary culture, adapting and assimilating many of its features while aiming at a distinctively Jewish

117

mode of expression. Hebrew grew both as an ethnic branch of Russian literature and as a counterculture.[1]

Historians are generally agreed that the Jewish problem in Tsarist Russia was inseparable from the general weaknesses of the empire. In a psychological sense, furthermore, the image of the Jew in Russian society and culture betrayed Russia's distorted self-image under the pressure of the need for rapid change. For to see the pogroms as isolated anti-Semitic outbursts is historically incorrect. They were, in fact, only a small fraction of the general unrest in Russia during the period, a symptom of the breakdown of Tsarist authority (Fuller, 1985; Klier and Lambroza, 1992). Challenged by the intelligentsia and the working masses alike, the government created the first modern police state, with extensive use of spying, repression and terror. In its dying days, despite an improving economy, the Tsarist empire had trouble feeding its large and growing population. It had the largest standing army in the world – about two and a half million – but to a degree unprecedented in history, the army was used to control and crush the internal opposition. In 1903, when the second wave of pogroms began, about one-third of its infantry and two-thirds of its cavalry were used against its own citizens (Fuller, 1985).

Nevertheless, the Jews more than most other ethnic groups suffered under Tsarist rule. Even prior to 1881 the Russian Jews were burdened with countless laws and restrictions. Most prominent was their confinement within the so-called Pale of Settlement on the western frontier of the empire. The pogroms brought about an 'ideological metamorphosis' away from adaptation and merging with Russia and in favour of mass emigration: 'spontaneously in almost every town of any size societies were founded for the colonization of Palestine' (Frankel, 1981, p. 49). The May Laws, passed in May 1882, which officially blamed the Jews for bringing the pogroms on their own heads, accentuated further their exclusion from Russian society. From then on, they were subjected to escalating waves of anti-Semitic violence and official discrimination. They left the territory of the empire in exceptionally large numbers. The majority – about two million in all – went to America, but two waves of these emigrants, totalling about 65,000, comprised the first *aliyot* (migrations to Palestine). The number of Jews who left Russia during this time comprised two-thirds of the total rate of emigration, though the Jews were less than 5 per cent of the empire's population.

For these reasons, 1881 is often regarded as the crucial date in modern Jewish history. Most significantly for the purposes of this book, 1881 roughly marks a point of *artistic* departure in modern Hebrew literature (Alter, 1988; Aberbach, 1993). The structural innovation in Russian Jewish politics after 1881 – its autonomy not only in relation to the state but also to the established Jewish leadership, which it now opposed (Frankel, 1981; Lederhendler, 1989) – was reflected in Hebrew literature. Prior to 1881, Russian Hebrew writers did not for the most part create works of enduring aesthetic value; after 1881 they did.

From the time of the freeing of the serfs in 1861 until 1917, the Russian Jews produced three different generations of writers and bodies of literature (though there was some overlapping), each representing a different mode of Jewish adaptation to the troubled Tsarist empire. The first, in Yiddish, was led by Mendele, whom we have encountered in the Introduction,[2] and by his younger contemporaries Sholom Aleichem (1859–1916)[3] and I.L. Peretz (1852–1915). Yiddish literature became to a large extent – unsuccessfully as it turned out – a vehicle for the survival of the Russian Jews as an ethnic minority within a clearly defined territory. A second, younger group consisted of assimilated Russian Jews – such as Isaac Babel, Osip Mandelstam, Boris Pasternak, Ilya Ehrenberg. These writers were born in the last years of the Pale of Settlement, abolished by the 1917 revolution. They rejected Yiddish and Hebrew in favour of Russian. Eventually they came to prominence as major Russian writers under Soviet rule.

The third group – the subject of this chapter – had the most far-reaching influence. It created a literary culture that acted as midwife to the birth of Zionism and the State of Israel. Hebrew literature of 1881–1917 was inseparable from the rise of political Zionism. Yet, the nationalism of this literature was Herderian in its primary concern with Jewish culture rather than with politics. Characteristic of this literary movement is the fact that Mendele, its leading writer of fiction, was contemptuous of political Zionism (Aberbach, 1993, pp. 45–6); Bialik, though hailed as the poet laureate of the Jewish national renaissance, persisted in writing deeply personal lyrics and neglected national themes (Aberbach, 1981, 1988); and Ahad Ha'am (1856–1927),[4] its outstanding theoretician, was locked in fierce debate with political Zionists in the years after 1897, when the World Zionist Organization was founded by Theodor Herzl (1860–1904). Other important Hebrew writers of the period, including David Frischmann (1859–1922), Gershom Shoffman (1880–1970), Zalman Schneour (1886–1959) and, above all, Uri Nissan Gnessin (1879–1913), were primarily interested in the creation of art rather than in having educational or political influence. This literature, in contrast with much pre-1881 Hebrew literature, attached great importance to childhood and to aggadah (Aberbach, 1995), to the exploration of the inner life of the individual, and to the creation of a distinct Jewish aesthetic as part of the developing national consciousness. Bialik and M.Y. Berdichevsky (1865–1921), who in many ways were ideological opponents, were agreed in their high valuation of aggadah: each produced anthologies of aggadah. Bialik's, edited jointly with Y. H. Ravnitsky (1908–11), has become a modern Hebrew classic. Berdichevsky's work has been undeservedly forgotten. As we have seen in the Introduction, the crucial spur in the Jewish national awakening was cultural. In this regard, it may be compared with other cultural nationalisms, including those of the Slovaks, the Greeks and the Irish (Hutchinson, 1987).

HISTORICAL AND LITERARY BACKGROUND

The background to the emergence of Hebrew cultural nationalism after 1881 has been touched on in the Introduction, but a few additional observations are apt here. During the 19th century, the Jewish population of Russia rose to nearly five million. It made up the largest, most homogeneous and dynamic, and most persecuted Jewish community of the time. The collapse of the Tsarist empire was by no means inevitable. Yet its weaknesses became clear with the fiasco of the Crimean War (1853–6). The freeing of the serfs in 1861 weakened the empire further by exacerbating its main problems: backwardness, social inequality, chronic poverty, unemployment and overcrowding in the cities. At the same time, autocratic rule was undermined by a new and growing university-educated intelligentsia and the limited introduction of capitalist-based industry. The failure of the Polish revolt of 1863 and the Russian–Turkish war of 1877–8 set off waves of Russian nationalism which, in turn, led to violent anti-Semitism. It may be that the use of Jew-hatred was not sanctioned officially as a diversion from revolutionary unrest within the empire (Rogger, 1986; Löwe, 1993); yet there is little doubt that the pogroms had this effect up to a point. Russian Judeophobia came by the end of the Reform Era, in 1881, 'to incorporate literally all of the fears and obsessions of a society in the midst of traumatic social change' (Klier, 1995, p. 455). There were two major waves of pogroms, in 1881–4 and 1903–6, in the Pale of Settlement. From the outbreak of pogroms in 1881 until the 1917 revolution, these circumstances stirred up a new Jewish national self-consciousness, with profound cultural and political consequences.

Hebrew literature prior to 1881 was a vital part of the background to the cultural nationalism of post-1881 Hebrew literature. The Odessa pogrom of 1871 was a significant turning point (Zipperstein, 1985; Haberer, 1995). Jewish intellectuals such as Mendele and Peretz Smolenskin (1842?–84) began at this time to question Haskalah ideals, and elements of Jewish nationalism entered Hebrew literature (Patterson, 1985). The leading Hebrew poet of the pre-1881 era, Judah Leib Gordon (1830–1892) – not Bialik – is cited by Kedourie (1960, pp. 100–1) as communicating in his poetry the alienation and the violent revolt against authority and restraints which are characteristic of national movements. The lexicographer Eliezer Ben-Yehuda tells in his autobiography (1917–18) that he conceived of Hebrew as a vehicle for Jewish nationalism in Palestine already in the late 1870s under the impact of the Russian nationalism stirred up by the Russian–Turkish war of 1877–8.

Nevertheless, prior to 1881 Hebrew literature was, for the most part, non-nationalistic, heavily didactic, artistically clumsy and linguistically shallow. The rise of Jewish nationalism after 1881 was a critical force galvanizing both the language and the literature. It brought the latter within a span of two generations into the front ranks of Western literature. (Samuel Joseph Agnon, the leading Hebrew novelist after Mendele's death in 1917, went on to win the Nobel Prize for Literature in 1966.) Hebrew in the Tsarist empire prior to 1881 had been used mainly as a catalyst for educational reform among the Jews and their assimilation (or 'russification') into Russian society. The 18th-century Age of Enlightenment and the liberal ideals promulgated by the French Revolution and spread by the Napoleonic wars had their Hebrew offshoot in the Haskalah (Enlightenment) movement. As in Germany and Galicia in the late 18th and early 19th centuries, Hebrew was adapted as the language by which the largely uneducated Jews could be introduced to the arts and sciences, particularly the latter. As long as Hebrew writers believed that emancipation and civil rights – above all the abolition of the Pale – were possible under Tsarist rule, they used Hebrew to promote secular education. The Russian Haskalah, lasting from the 1820s to 1881, was the springboard for post-1881 Hebrew literature. It inspired much translation of educational works as well as experiments in poetry, drama and autobiography. It created the first Hebrew novels, starting with Abraham Mapu's *Ahavat Tziyon* (The Love of Zion, 1853) and included influential works by Gordon (Stanislawski, 1988), Smolenskin, Mendele, Braudes and others (Patterson, 1964). Though this work has scant artistic merit, its historical importance is vast. Its relationship with post-1881 Hebrew literature brings to mind Saltykov-Shchedrin's fable of the ram troubled by a word (freedom) which it cannot clearly remember. The Jews in the same way were dimly aware of a viable national identity beyond Russia's borders: the pogroms were the main trauma bringing it to consciousness.

THE POGROMS AND HEBREW LITERATURE

The pogroms which broke out after the assassination of Tsar Alexander II in 1881 were the death-blow to Haskalah ideology and the hope of Jewish emancipation under Tsarist rule. After 1881, Hebrew literature was inseparably part of a critical mass of national feeling, of will and creativity liberated by trauma and the new realism which followed. Hebrew writers no longer used Hebrew literature primarily to teach the ideology of assimilation and Russian patriotism. They aimed instead to depict Jewish life as they saw it, for its own sake and with empathy. Apart from the already mentioned fiction of Mendele, poems of Bialik and essays of Ahad Ha'am, the high points of their achievement include: four short novels by Gnessin; a group of semi-fictional autobiographies by Mendele, Bialik, M.Z. Feierberg (1875–99), J. H. Brenner (1881–1921) and Berdichevsky; poems by Saul Tchernichowsky (1875–1943); and the Hebrew translations of Sholom Aleichem's stories by I.D. Berkowitz (1885–1973) and the Hebrew translations (by Peretz and others) of Peretz's stories. The chief literary characters in Hebrew at the turn of the century, Mendele the Bookpeddler and Sholom Aleichem's Tevye the Dairyman – both tragi-comic creations – are without precedent or parallel in Jewish or any other literature. Interestingly, these characters are based on Yiddish originals, but they became inseparably a part of Hebrew literature.

The bulk of this work, comprising a dozen or so volumes in all, was published in the 15 years between 1896 and 1911. Rarely in literary history have a literature and language undergone such massive change as Hebrew did in this short time.

This literature has a unique socio-linguistic character. Its writers were all native Yiddish speakers. Their leader was Mendele who had a seminal role as the 'grandfather' both of modern Yiddish and Hebrew fiction. His novels, most of which were written twice, first in Yiddish and then in Hebrew, were the principal achievement in Hebrew prose fiction prior to 1939. Two of these Yiddish works, *Die Kliatsche* (The Mare, 1873) and *Masos Binyomin ha-Shlishi* (The Travels of Benjamin the Third, 1878), pre-date 1881; the latter, published in 1896, became the first classic in modern Hebrew. Mendele was the first to recognize in Yiddish a catalyst for the creation of lasting art in Hebrew. Mendele's novels are mostly set during the reign of Nicholas I, and the Hebrew drafts post-date the Yiddish ones by as much as thirty years and more (e.g. *The Mare*); yet, the basic conditions of the Russian Jews in the time of Nicholas II, when all the Hebrew drafts were written, were little better than they had been a half-century previously. Consequently, they largely retained their social relevance after 1881.

Unlike post-1948 Hebrew writers, Hebrew writers of 1881–1917 were self-taught intellectuals, mostly without even a high school diploma. Almost all were lapsed from a religious background and had intensive experience of rabbinical seminaries (*yeshivot*), where they were for the most part outstanding scholars. Their alienation from traditional Judaism and their struggle to adapt to a new, secular world are central motifs in their autobiographical works (Mintz, 1989). The richness of their style, at its best, reflects years of study. They brought a religious fervour and reverence for the Hebrew language in adapting its classical idioms to modern secular art. Perhaps the closest literary analogue to this aspect of their achievement is James Joyce's *Ulysses*. They denied through mock-heroic satire the sacred authority of the sources but implicitly accepted their imperishable value and their power to inspire (Aberbach, 1993).

HEBREW AND JEWISH LIBERATION

The metamorphosis of Hebrew after the pogroms of 1881–2 helped to bring about political metamorphosis via the Zionist Organization in which the Russian Jews soon became the largest and most influential group. Zionism promoted Hebrew as the national language of all Jews and the growth of creative literature in Hebrew as an integral part of the national renaissance. The sudden, steep rise in the status and artistic value of Hebrew literature would have been highly unlikely had the Russian empire been stronger and less gripped by Jew-hatred. Jewish literature became a vehicle for a form of emigration into a private national domain, the full dimensions of which would soon be mapped out.

While there was and could be no open call for revolution, a number of new features of Hebrew literature were revolutionary: Bialik's revival of the biblical prophetic style, bitter, angry and critical of the status quo, striking in imagery and rhythmic power, demanding truth and justice; Berdichevsky's call for the Nietzschean release of the instinctual power of the individual; the proud dionysiac assertiveness of Schneour's poetry; Tchernichowsky's idealization of the Greek way of life, its heroes and mythology, whose healthy, democratic nature implicitly contrasted with the repression of Tsarist rule and the stifling narrowness of Russian Jewish life; the introduction of the heretic as a sympathetic character in the writings of Feierberg, Brenner, Berdichevsky and others. The defiant spirit of the age is, perhaps, best captured in Bialik's poems, such as *En zot ki rabat tzerartunu* (Nothing but your fierce hounding, 1899):

> Nothing but your fierce hounding
> has turned us into beasts of prey!
> With cruel fury
> we'll drink your blood.
> We'll have no pity
> when the whole nation rises, cries –
> 'Revenge!'

Not least, the elevation of the common Jew as a subject of serious Hebrew literary art, rather than to promote an educational message, was revolutionary: it began with Mendele's act of introducing the character of Mendele the Bookpeddler into a Hebrew story in 1886, after over two decades of depicting this character exclusively in Yiddish fiction (Aberbach, 1993). This act implicitly rejected the idea of inborn superiority, for even ordinary Yiddish-speaking Jews – a bookseller, a bath-house attendant or beggar – could be presented artistically and with human significance. This literature counteracted the dehumanization of the Jews resulting from anti-Semitic violence, poverty and discrimination.

The disdain which Russian-Jewish intellectuals previously felt for the ignorant, superstitious Jewish masses now largely disappeared. It was replaced by warm and curious, though not uncritical, sympathy. The populist movement in Russia in the late 1870s, with its idealization of the Russian peasant, also left its mark on Jewish literary self-perceptions. Even the ultra-Orthodox pious Jews, the *Hasidim*, who throughout the 19th century had served as the chief satiric target in Hebrew (Davidson, 1966), were now described far more seriously (in Peretz's collection of stories, *Hasidut*, with glowing empathy), as repositories of profound folk wisdom.

The waves of pogroms of 1881–4 and 1903–6 liberated the Hebrew language and literature in specific practical ways. Emigration to Palestine triggered off by the pogroms brought about the creation of hundreds of Hebrew-speaking groups in Russia. Suddenly, it became clear to the young Russian Jewish men and women who were thinking of emigrating that the emerging Jewish community in Palestine was the most heterogeneous in the world: only one language united its varied groups – Hebrew.

The pogroms were the catalyst for a historic encounter between the Russian Jewish lower middle class and the Hebrew intelligentsia, leading to a phenomenal increase in Hebrew journalism and in Hebrew readers, which may have reached 100,000 already in the 1880s (Miron, 1987, p. 59ff.). For the first time, Hebrew writers could, in theory, make a living from their writings, and publishers could make substantial profits. In the short story *Bi-Yme ha-Ra'ash* (In Stormy Days, 1890), Mendele gives a brilliant satiric picture of the time: a bedraggled *melamed* attempting to escape the pogroms to Palestine via Odessa is converted literally overnight into a private tutor of modern Hebrew. The upsurge of interest in the study and creation of modern spoken Hebrew and journalism naturally increased the market for creative Hebrew. As a result, the artistic standard of this literature rose impressively after 1881. Hebrew readers of important writers such as Mendele, Bialik, Brenner and Gnessin during this period rarely exceeded a few thousand, but this was far more than during the pre-1881 period. These readers constituted an elite, widely read and discerning, though mostly self-taught, and familiar with European and Russian literature. Hebrew literature, previously imitative, became competitive. It now aimed, largely successfully, to become an important part of European literature. The optimism and didacticism of Haskalah literature were turned round. Much post-1881 Hebrew literature is pessimistic and anxiety-ridden, foreshadowing the tone of post-First World War European literature. Yet, this literature also includes two outstanding humourists – Mendele and Sholom Aleichem (again, in Berkowitz's translation) – who convey a Yiddish comic sensibility which, in retrospect, appears to have been virtually a condition of survival in the Pale. As mentioned previously, Mendele's comic novella *The Travels of Benjamin the Third* was recast from a Yiddish original of 1878. However, it is highly significant in considering 1881 as a psychological divide in Jewish history and literature that whereas in the Yiddish draft of *The Travels* the quixotic Benjamin does not reach Palestine, in the Hebrew draft of 1896 he does. In the Hebrew version, Benjamin emerges in the end more as a courageous visionary than an unbalanced figure of fun.

Following the 1903 pogrom in Kishinev, Bialik developed a programme of *kinnus*, the 'ingathering' of fragments of Jewish culture in an effort to give new force and direction to the growing Jewish national consciousness. *Kinnus* found practical expression in Bialik's work as a publisher and his co-editing of the legends and folklore of the Talmud and Midrash, as well as of the medieval Hebrew poetry of Solomon Ibn Gabirol and Moses Ibn Ezra. But his poems, particularly the prophetic 'poems of wrath', are themselves a major contribution to *kinnus*, a harmonious amalgam of Hebrew strata parallel to Mendele's achievement in prose.

Maxim Gorky, who read the 'poems of wrath' in Russian translation, called Bialik a modern Isaiah. Most of these poems were written during and in response to the pogroms of 1903–6. They express the outrage and impotence felt by the Russian Jews as well as the aggressiveness which led to increased militancy, especially among the young. It is estimated that by 1903 about half of those arrested for revolutionary activities in Russia were Jews. The official tendency to identify revolutionaries with 'the Jews' – though the vast majority of Russian Jews were not – is exemplified in a letter of Tsar Nicholas II to his mother on 27 October 1905: 'nine-tenths of the revolutionaries are Yids' (in Pipes, 1990, p. 48). Bialik's 'poems of wrath' are the outstanding literary expression of the growing radicalization of the post-1881 generation (Aberbach, 1988). They mark a turning point in modern Jewish history, the beginning of a far-reaching change in Jewish consciousness and the emergence from powerlessness:

As our voices entreating lift into the darkness –
Whose ear will turn?
As our raw blasphemy streams to heaven –
Over whose crown will it trickle?
Grinding tooth, knuckling ire-veined fists –
On whose scalp will the fury drift?
all will fall windily
Down the throat of chaos;
No comfort remains, no helping hand, no way out –
And heaven is dumb;
Murdering us with dispassionate eyes,
Bearing its blame in blood-torn silence.

Davar (1904)

The art which Russian Jewish writers created from then until the revolution is built upon the conviction of holding the moral high ground. Their alienation from Russia, painful though it was, forced them to break from Russia and from the ideology of assimilation, to seek inner sources of strength and freedom. The following lines from Feierberg's novella *Le'an?* (Whither? 1899), though put into the mouth of a madman, sums up the metamorphosis which turned many disillusioned young Russian Jews back to their semitic roots and to Palestine:

The greatest enemy that Judaism has ever had has been... the West, which is why I believe it to be unnatural that we Hebrews, we Easterners, should throw in our lot with the West as we set out for the East... I believe that this great people, without whose books and spiritual genius the world could not possibly have achieved what it has, will again give a new civilization to the human race, but this civilization will be Eastern.

(1973, p. 214)

HEBREW AND RUSSIAN LITERATURE

As pointed out earlier, 19th-century Hebrew literature was closely linked with contemporary Russian literature. In some respects, including its countercultural qualities, it might be regarded almost as a branch of Russian literature. The Russian and Hebrew writers came from radically different social and religious backgrounds. The

first group was largely aristocratic and wealthy, the second mostly
from impoverished homes. Yet they lived in the same empire at the
same time. They describe the same general world and confront
similar problems. Revulsion at the poverty, backwardness and
injustice of life in Tsarist Russia was common to Russian as to
Hebrew and Yiddish literature. Each of these literatures explores
social and psychological malaises which contributed to the break-up
of the Tsarist empire. The humane depiction of the ordinary Jew in
late 19th-century Hebrew fiction – a phenomenon which began
before 1881, though initially without lasting artistry – was as revolutionary as that of the Russian peasants in Turgenev's *Notes of a
Huntsman* (1852).

   The quarter-century rule of Alexander II (1855–81) produced an
unrivalled body of Russian prose fiction, including *Fathers and Sons*
(1861), *Crime and Punishment* (1865–6), *War and Peace* (1865–8), *Anna
Karenina* (1874–6) and *The Brothers Karamazov* (1880). The subtlety
and depth of Russian literature, its moral power, the astonishing
variety of its great characters, its heady blend of realism, idealism
and universalism, its potential subversiveness – and its anti-Semitism – all left their mark on Hebrew literature. No Hebrew writer
equalled Tolstoy or Dostoevsky. Chekhov, a major influence on
the generation of Hebrew writers born around the 1881 watershed
(Gnessin, Shoffman, Brenner), is far and away their superior as an
artist, as they themselves would have admitted, notwithstanding
their crucial importance in the development of modern Hebrew
fiction. For inasmuch as these writers set Russian literature as their
chief model for the depiction of modern life, they inevitably came
off second. Hebrew at the time was still too wooden and
undeveloped. However, some Hebrew writers, notably Mendele
and Bialik, adopted Western literary standards while creating a
new style of Hebrew based on the full richness of the Hebrew
literary tradition. (Often they did this after writing a first draft in
Yiddish.) These writers had far greater artistic success. Mendele's
dual achievement in Yiddish as well as Hebrew is comparable with
that of Gogol or Turgenev, certainly of Saltykov-Shchedrin. Bialik's
best poetry is not inferior to that of Lermontov or the young
Pushkin. Characters such as Benjamin the Third or Tevye the
Dairyman, both recast from Yiddish originals, are indigenous to
Russia: though they are manifestly Jewish, Russia (or, to be more
specific, the Ukraine) is their native soil. Also, as a charismatic
literary figure in the Jewish national movement, Bialik had an

influence on Russian Jewish society which was in some ways even greater than that of Tolstoy on Russian society (Aberbach, 1996).

Perhaps at no other time was a secular literature valued so highly among its readers – to the point of acting as a compass of moral direction and social and political change – as in Russia in the second half of the 19th century. For the Russian-Jewish intelligentsia, this view of literature came easily, with the Bible and Talmud as its precedent. The Russian perception of literature as a means of changing society was largely adapted by Hebrew writers, though by the 1890s the 'art for art's sake' movement affected both literatures.

The two often overlapping streams of Hebrew literature, one drawing from native Jewish culture and the other from Western influences, are closely paralleled in the two main directions of Russian literature, the Slavophile and the Western. As in Russian literature, notably the fiction of Ivan Bunin, the village, or *shtetl*, became a stock setting of Hebrew literature, often treated with contempt, or in a sentimental or semi-satirical style. Gogol's description in *Dead Souls* (1842) of the 'quixotic' element in the Russian character is duplicated among the Russian Jews: Mendele's *Travels of Benjamin the Third*, as indicated earlier, tells of a Jewish Quixote who sets off with his Sancho Panza for the Holy Land. Mendele's satiric juxtapositions of biblical and talmudic characters and allusions with contemporary realities bring to mind similarly absurd juxtapositions in Russian literature, for example, in Leskov's 'Lady Macbeth of Mtsensk' or Turgenev's 'A Hamlet of the Shchigry District'. The character of the 'superfluous man' and the *talush* ('uprooted') is common to both literatures: the man with gifts which have no outlet, alienated and trapped in conditions over which he has little control.

Russian and Jewish literatures of the late Tsarist period are united in their critical attitude to the role of education in a society in which the dominant problem was getting enough to eat from day to day (Aberbach, 1993, pp. 80–2). The purpose of education, both secular and religious, is called into question. The most striking poetic expression in Hebrew of being at an educational crossroads is Bialik's *Lifne aron hasefarim* (In front of the bookcase, 1910). The poet stands in front of a bookcase whose sacred books no longer meet present-day needs. This scene echoes Chekhov's *The Cherry Orchard* (1904), though without the comic irony, when Gayev addresses the family bookcase. Gayev and his family are about to lose their estate through bankruptcy. The bookcase is a symbol of loss, not only of the property but of noble ideals identical with those of the Haskalah:

> Dear bookcase! Most esteemed bookcase! I salute your existence, which for more than a hundred years now has been directed towards the shining ideals of goodness and truth. For a hundred years your unspoken summons to fruitful labour has never faltered, upholding [*in tears*] through all the generations of our family, wisdom and faith in a better future, and fostering within us ideals of goodness and of social consciousness.
>
> (1975, p. 13)

The radical critique of orthodox religion is another feature which binds Russian and Hebrew literature in an age of imperial decline. This critique was especially vehement prior to 1881, when Haskalah ideology emerged in opposition to what was often seen as a stifling puritan tradition based on outmoded rabbinic authority. In some cases, the attacks on the rabbis may have been unnaturally severe because the Jewish clergy, in common with the Russian orthodox priests, represented the status quo and, therefore, became symbolic of oppressive authority. The rabbis, like some of the priests in Russian literature, were acceptable targets for social criticism and satire, unlike the totalitarian government which had subjected the Jews to hundreds of restrictive laws. The anti-clericalism of Hebrew literature remained after 1881 but in a toned-down fashion as the Jews were galvanized into unprecedented unity by Christian hatred.

Censorship deeply affected both Hebrew and Russian literature. It made open criticism of the government impossible and encouraged self-blame and self-hate. Jewish writers, intentionally or not, resorted to displacements or, following the lead of Saltykov-Shchedrin, used an 'Aesopic' language of fables to hint at their intentions. In the greatest of these allegories, Mendele's *The Mare*, the battered mare is a symbol of the Jewish people whose miserable state is caused by prejudice and discrimination. However, when it came to the question of blame, the Jews are themselves held responsible for the mare's pathetic state. In much the same way, Gogol, in his tale of Captain Kopeikin in *Dead Souls*, was forced by the censors to alter his attacks on the uncaring Tsarist bureaucracy that denied a soldier mutilated in war a proper pension. Instead, he put the blame for Kopeikin's misfortune on Kopeikin, not on the authorities.

In Hebrew as in Russian literature both before and after 1881, censorship taxed the ingenuity of the writer, to convey a desired meaning subtly and allusively. In this way, Hebrew writers such as Bialik discovered that the resources of Jewish history and literature gave cover to thoughts and emotions which would otherwise have been banned. The poem quoted above beginning 'Nothing but your fierce hounding' got past the censor as it was originally called 'Bar-Kokhba,' which set it safely in the 2nd century CE.

Any challenge to authority was politically charged both in Hebrew and Russian literature. Under the Tsarist regime, literature became a vital outlet by which the depiction of individual consciousness was indirectly an act of rebellion against a social system in which there was scarcely room for individualism. The idea expressed by Ivan Karamazov in Dostoevsky's *The Brothers Karamazov* that 'If God is dead, all things are possible' is implicit in Hebrew literature. Bialik's poem *Al ha-Shehitah* (On the Slaughter), written after the Kishinev pogrom in 1903, questions the existence of God, apparently for the first time in Hebrew:

> Heaven, beg mercy for me –
> If you have a God and he can be found –
> pray for me!

In Feierberg's *Whither?*, the hero's break from the authority of family and religion, as well as his incipient Zionism, is signalled by the momentous act of blowing out a candle in the synagogue on Yom Kippur. If such sacrilege is possible, then anything is possible – even the overthrow of the Tsar, the restoration of the Jews to their ancestral homeland, and the revival of Hebrew language and literature.

HEBREW LITERARY STEREOTYPES

Perhaps the most striking and important similarity in Hebrew and Russian literature is the low opinion – often coupled with great affection – the writers of each language appear to have of their own people (Aberbach, 1993). This aspect of Russian literature may be taken to presage the need for revolution; in Hebrew literature it is part of Jewish self-criticism accompanying the national revival. Almost every Jewish literary stereotype crops up in Mendele's writings. Though vile and expressive at times of Jewish self-hate, these stereotypes are exploded through empathy and the passion for social change. They are seen as a symptom, not a cause, of poverty and backwardness whose elimination would allow a new type of Jew, free, strong and confident, to emerge. For this reason, though not a political Zionist, Mendele was adopted by the Zionist camp. His writings, with their ambivalence towards and satire of diaspora Jews, were interpreted as a justification of Zionism.[5]

Mendele's ambivalence towards his own people is often expressed in the pose of the impartial entomological observer. Like a natural scientist – in the 1860s and 1870s he had produced the first *Natural History* in Hebrew – the narrator of his stories constantly likens the Jews to ants or fleas. For example, in Mendele's fictional autobiography *Ba-Yammim ha-Hem* (Of Bygone Days, 1894, 1903–17), mostly recast from a Yiddish original of the same period, the narrator complains: 'We are a congregation – no, a heap – of ants. In a book on natural history you find a chapter on ants, not on any one ant' (1947, p. 259). In *Ha-Nisrafim* (The Fire Victims, 1897), an indigent Jew complains to Mendele the Bookpeddler that the house of study where he slept has burned down in a fire which destroyed the whole town – this often happened in Russia – and Mendele cruelly remarks to himself: 'Fleas if they could talk would argue so after losing their lodgings in houses and beds' (*ibid.* p. 445). Blatant anti-Semitic stereotyping occurs frequently in Mendele's description of typical Jewish noses, the Jews' uncleanliness and unhygienic manners, their ridiculous appearance and love of money.

Russian literature prior to the 1880s was full of similar anti-Semitic stereotyping, though without the empathy and reforming zeal which mark Mendele's fiction far more strongly than self-hate. Lermontov's play *The Spaniards*, Turgenev's story 'The Jew', Gogol's novels *Taras Bulba* and *Dead Souls*, Dostoevsky's fictional memoir *The House of the Dead* (1860), the satires of Saltykov-Shchedrin, Tolstoy's *Anna Karenina*, among others, betray shameful prejudice and hatred nourished by the Church and kept alive in the popular imagination. Whatever their personal views of the Jewish people, pre-1881 Russian writers fell short of their liberal, humanistic ideals when they wrote of Jews. The literary stereotype built largely on Church anti-Semitism poisoned the image of living Jews. In *The House of the Dead*, Dostoevsky tells of the Jew whom he met while imprisoned in Siberia:

> He was the only Jew in our barrack, and even now I cannot recall him without laughing. Every time I looked at him I would think of the Jew Yankel in Gogol's *Taras Bulba* who, when he undressed

in order to climb, together with his Jewess, into some sort of cupboard, looked uncommonly like a chicken.

(1965, p. 93)

The anti-Semitism here as elsewhere in Dostoevsky's major writings is muted in comparison with the virulent hatred spewed out in his publicistic works (Goldstein, 1981).

Perhaps the most disturbing and dangerous side to this literary stereotype was the fact that while most Russian Jews lived in conditions of unspeakable poverty and degradation, Russian literature persisted in depicting 'the Jew' as being wealthy and in the habit of using his wealth to oppress Russians. Russian writers prior to 1881 seem to have been largely unable to contemplate a Jew without medieval associations of moneylending, miserliness, trickery and extortion. In *Dead Souls*, for example, Chichikov tries to persuade Nozdryov to sell his dead souls and Nozdryov, sensing a trick, keeps urging him to buy something of value: 'what Jewish instincts you have,' thinks Chichikov (p. 89). The Jewish revolutionary Liamshin in Dostoevsky's *The Devils* (1871–2) is singled out as a traitor to Russia, a new Judas (Goldstein, 1981), though Jewish involvement in the Russian revolutionary movement at this time was minimal. Even in *Anna Karenina* the only Jewish character is presented stereotypically. Prince Oblonsky covets a lucrative post on the railway board and is kept waiting to his annoyance by Bulgarinov, a Jew whose support he needs (1968, p. 775).

A measure of the extraordinarily poor image of the Jew in Russian society prior to 1881 (and, to a large extent, afterwards) is that although these Russian works are counted among the classics in world literature and are peopled with a wide range of characters, the negative image of the Jew is the only one which appears in them. There are no realistic or even sympathetic portraits to balance them, as for example Riah in Dickens' *Our Mutual Friend* is a corrective to Fagin in *Oliver Twist*. Jewish nationalism and the accompanying creation of a vibrant Hebrew literature became a means of fighting this racist stereotype by means of more balanced self-portrayals.

RUSSIAN LITERARY STEREOTYPES

The distorted perception of the Jews is in most respects equalled by the generally low view of the Russian people in Russian literature.

This sense of inferiority made the Russians especially vulnerable (as were the Germans in the 1920s and 1930s) to the projective identification of anti-Semitism. The self-hatred expressed by the characters in Russian literature (who in some cases are authorial mouthpieces) might be seen as foreshadowings of the collapse of the Romanov empire inasmuch as it implicitly calls for radical change. This self-image is reflected in Hebrew literature of 1881– 1917. Bazarov puts it succinctly in Turgenev's *Fathers and Sons*: 'The only good thing about a Russian is the poor opinion he has of himself' (1965, p. 116). Gogol's particular genius was to delineate with sharp, precise strokes of satire this allegedly inferior side of the Russian character.[6] It is uncanny how closely Mendele's satires against the Jews resemble the jibes at the Russians in Gogol's works, notably in *Dead Souls*: 'no Russian likes to admit before others that he is to blame' (p. 99); 'You know perfectly well what a Russian peasant is like: settle him on new land and set him to till it, with nothing prepared for him, neither cottage nor farmstead, and, well, he'll run away, as sure as twice two makes four' (p. 164); 'In general, we somehow don't seem to be made for representative assemblies' (p. 208); 'a Russian is wise after the event' (p. 215); 'a Russian likes spicy words; he needs them as much as a glass of vodka for his digestion' (p. 307); 'A Russian, to judge by myself, cannot carry on without a taskmaster: otherwise he will only drowse off and go to seed' (p. 339). The contempt which Jewish writers often felt for the Yiddish language had its parallel in the disdain which the Russian intelligentsia had for Russian. As the narrator puts it sarcastically in *Dead Souls*:

> To ennoble the Russian tongue even more, almost half its words were banished from their conversation, and because of that they had very often to have recourse to French.
>
> (p. 169)

Russia's weaknesses were betrayed in her perception and treatment of the Jews and in the Jews' vulnerability. It is a lesson of history that a nation's Jewish policy is a gauge of its self-image. The psychologist Erik Erikson has described how individuals belonging to a hated minority might in any case come to hate their own people:

> The individual belonging to an oppressed and exploited minority which is aware of the dominant cultural ideals but prevented

from emulating them, is apt to fuse the negative images held up to him by the dominant majority with the negative identity cultivated in his own group.

(1974, p. 303)

The 'negative images' are likely to be all the more vicious if the dominant majority has a strongly negative self-image. Indeed, it is striking how the main criticisms of Russia in Russian literature are echoed in pre-1881 Hebrew literature: for example, in the charges of the lack of dignity, parasitism, backwardness and demonic corruption. Prior to 1881, the attacks on Jewish society in Hebrew (and Yiddish) literature are mainly a clarion for social reform; after 1881, for national revival. In his letter to Gogol of 1847, for example, Belinsky writes that what Russia needs is 'the reawakening in the people of a sense of their human dignity lost for so many centuries amid the dirt and refuse' (1981, p. 537). A similar attitude prevailed among enlightened Jews toward the Jewish masses in the Pale of Settlement. In *Dead Souls*, likewise, the charge of parasitism is implicitly levelled by Gogol against the privileged classes, the landowners and the bureaucracy who treat human beings like property. Identical charges against the Jewish upper class appear frequently in nineteenth-century Yiddish and Hebrew literature (for example, in Mendele's novel *Dos Kleyne Mentschele* (The Parasite, 1864–5). The critic Chernyshevsky's attack in the 1840s upon the total lack of originality in Russian intellectual life – 'What have the Russians given to learning? Alas, nothing. What has learning contributed to Russian life? Again, nothing' (in Treadgold, 1973, p. 181) – is echoed in the critique of traditional Jewish life in Haskalah literature. Turgenev went so far in his novel *Smoke* as to suggest that if Russia were destroyed it would be no great loss to civilization.

The low national self-image in Russian literature, though not unmixed with pride and empathy, came largely out of the awareness that most of the empire's population was desperately poor and ignorant. The disgust and condescension often felt by educated Russians toward the peasants is well expressed in Dostoevsky's *Crime and Punishment*, set shortly after the liberation of the serfs in 1861. The examining magistrate Porphyry jokes sardonically with Raskolnikov that no educated murderer would take refuge in the Russian countryside: 'our modern educated Russian would sooner be in jail than live among such foreigners as our peasants' (1966, p. 355). In *The House of the Dead*, Dostoevsky expresses amazement at the number of literate prisoners among whom he was incarcerated for four years in Omsk, Siberia, in the early 1850s:

> In what other place where ordinary Russians are gathered together in large numbers would you be able to find a group of two hundred and fifty men, half of whom could read and write?
>
> (1985, p. 31)

Even the idea that the Jews are in some way possessed by the Devil, in Mendele's *The Mare* as in the traditional anti-Jewish stereotype, is echoed in Russian literature of the same period. At the end of Dostoevsky's *The Devils*, the dying progressive scholar Stepan Verhovensky retells the New Testament story of the devils entering the swine as a parable of contemporary Russia:

> That's exactly like our Russia, those devils that come out of the sick man and enter into the swine. They are the sores, all the foul contagions, all the impurities, all the devils great and small that have multiplied in that great invalid, our beloved Russia, in the course of ages and ages.
>
> (1952, II, p. 288)

This roughly corresponded with Dostoevsky's own view of Russia, the germ of his novel which, he wrote in a letter of 9/21 October 1870 to A.N. Maikov, 'describes how the devils entered into the herd of swine' (1987, p. 343).

Not surprisingly, then, Russia's leading satirist of the late nineteenth century, Saltykov-Shchedrin, who influenced Mendele in his satiric portrayal of towns such as Glupsk and in beast fables such as *The Mare* – he used the battered mare as a symbol of the exploited Russian peasant – took a deeply negative view of Russian society and institutions, which he characterized as being ruled by 'arbitrariness, hypocrisy, lying, rapacity, and vacuity' (1986, p. vii).

A further sign that Russian Jewish writers often took their cue from Russian writers may be seen in the fact that when Russian writers, in part because they were shocked by the pogroms of 1881–2, began to depict Jews favourably – for example, in works by Leskov, Chekhov, Korolenko and Gorky – the image of the Jew in Mendele and other Jewish writers became markedly less satirical and more realistic and positive. The negative image in Hebrew literature, as in Russian, might represent on one level a breaking away from this image, a declaration of 'not us', a function not unlike that of anti-Semitic literary stereotypes in Russian and other literatures. This splitting away from disapora Jewry, which was perhaps inevitable in the creation of a new national identity, has resulted to this day in a deeply ambivalent Israeli view of the diaspora.

CONCLUSION

Hebrew literature of 1881–1917 in some ways marks a revolutionary point of departure both from previous Hebrew literature (and, indeed, from Judaism and the predominantly sacred Hebrew literature of the past) and also, in its assertion of Jewish distinctiveness, from Russian and European literature. At the same time, the social and political causes which forged Hebrew into an artistic instrument for Jewish cultural nationalism also gave Russian literature its revolutionary impetus. The extraordinary artistic quality of Hebrew literature of this period must be ascribed to the convergence of cultural influences in which each major stratum of Hebrew literature in the past and much of the most important 19th-century world literature played their part. Imitation came to serve the cause of Jewish national assertion. The growth of European nationalism and anti-Semitism in the latter part of the 19th century drove many of the Russian Jews to rediscover their religious-cultural roots while rejecting traditional clerical authority. In doing so, they redefined their national identity by asserting a new aggressive creativity, mainly through massive development of literary and spoken Hebrew. This revival of an ancient language has no parallel in cultural history. Following its meteoric ascent, in 1881–1917, Hebrew was exiled by the Soviet empire, driven back to its birthplace and only homeland. In the Land of Israel, Hebrew has continued as a critical mouthpiece for Jewish national identity. It has grown with confidence and creative vigour lacking since the time of the Bible.

Notes

INTRODUCTION

1. Sáenz-Badillos describes the fundamental unity which the Hebrew Bible has given Hebrew language and literature throughout its history:

   The language has remained substantially the same down the years, undergoing changes that have appreciably affected its vocabulary but not, on the whole, its essential morphological, phonological, or even syntactic structure. The truth of this statement even extends to the Hebrew spoken and written today, following a fascinating process of revival. The fundamental unity of Hebrew, both its language and its literature, is beyond doubt. Not only have the basic structures of the language, its morphological system, and especially its verbal morphology, been preserved without major changes over the centuries, but it is also possible to claim that the vocabulary of the Bible has been the basis for all later periods, despite the numerous innovations of each era.

   (1993, p. 50)

2. For a history of Jewish literature from the 'golden age' of Muslim Spain to the 20th century, see Zinberg (1929–37). Also see separate entries in the *Encyclopedia Judaica*. A representative anthology of Hebrew poetry from the Bible to the present is that of Carmi (1981). Copious translation from the prophets is given by Aberbach (1993). The outstanding literary anthology of aggadah from the Talmud and Midrash is that of Bialik and Ravnitsky (1992). The 'golden age' of medieval Hebrew poetry is well-represented in Goldstein (1965). Two excellent anthologies of modern Hebrew prose fiction are edited by Alter (1975) and Abramson (1996). The role of social and political crisis in stimulating important literature has been noted by sociologists. Goldmann, for instance, writes: 'On the social as well as the individual plane, it is the sick organ which creates awareness, and it is in periods of crisis that men are most aware of the enigma of their presence in the world' (1964, p. 49). On the sociology of Jewish languages, including a number of essays on Hebrew, see Fishman (1985). With regard to sociological study of Hebrew in the context of empires, the present work is unique. Indeed, the sociological study of literature is itself a relatively recent phenomenon. See Laurenson and Swingewood (1972) and Hall (1979). According to Hall, 'One of the greatest weaknesses of the traditional sociology of literature has been its inability to specify the exact links between literature and sociology' (p. 24).

3. Much of the oral literature of the *tannaim* apparently survived verbatim until it was written down. (See Chapter 2, note 1 below.) It was treated as sacred and preserved for a number of reasons, some of which may be listed: (a) the *tannaim* attached the highest importance to Hebrew as *lashon kodesh* (the holy tongue), and the main body of sayings attributed to them is in Hebrew; (b) their oral tradition was itself classified as Torah, whose every letter was regarded as holy; (c) the *tannaim* had immense prestige as they were perceived by later generations as having saved Judaism after the destruction of the Temple. Post-*tannaic* rabbis (*amoraim*) do not generally disagree with *tannaim* unless there is a Mishnaic

support for their views; (d) the *tannaim* fixed the biblical canon in which only Hebrew works were included, they standardized the prayers, again in Hebrew, and they created an educational system, again in which Hebrew was at the core of the curriculum; (e) they addressed with great insight and originality the humiliating trauma of defeat and exile, the effects of which lasted in some ways indefinitely; (f) many of the *tannaim* were martyrs in defence of their faith, and their memory and sayings were treasured. It may be that much *tannaic* literature was written at the time, as suggested in the *Tosefta* and the *Avot de-Rabbi Nathan*, where Rabbi Akiva is credited with editing an earlier version of the Mishna. See Lieberman (1962). As indicated in the Introduction above, the *tannaim* compiled the surviving midrashim on the Bible, and 'particular passages in these texts can usually be dated by the rabbis said to participate in them' (Goodman, 1983, p. 11). It is true that Hebrew literature of the *tannaic* period might not have been actually written down at the time, but this is irrelevant to the universally recognized fact that post-Mishnaic Midrash and aggadah, as well as halakhah, derive their creative impetus and authority largely from the period 66–200 CE. For these reasons, most of the rabbis cited in this chapter are those believed to have lived during the period 66–200 CE. Later rabbis are occasionally quoted to illustrate ideas which might be related to the *tannaic* age. It should be emphasized, however, that *tannaic* literature does not form a unified corpus, nor does it tell what all Jews thought and felt at the time. Yet it derives in large part from a trauma experienced by all Jews and with lasting influence on the collective Jewish psyche and on the development of Judaism. For a selection of early rabbinic texts, see Maccoby (1988). A brief, concise overview of the period in which the Mishna evolved after 70 CE is given by Goodman in the forthcoming second edition of *Cambridge Ancient History*, vol. XI.

4. Following the line of argument that the most notable advances in Hebrew literature are linked with severe political and social crisis, it is highly significant that the emergence of the Hebrew prayerbook was spurred on by the decline of Babylonian Jewry in the 8th–10th centuries, the disappearance of the Gaonate by the 11th century and the demographic shift during this time of large numbers of Jews from the east to North Africa and Europe. See, for example, Reif (1993) and Petuchowski (1978). Also see Chapter 3, p. 97.

5. The Austro-Hungarian Jews of the 1881–1917 period were far more assimilated than the Russian Jews and their main language was German rather than Yiddish. Their chief contribution to literature was in German, not Hebrew or Yiddish, in the writings of Altenberg, Beer-Hofmann, Hofmannsthal, Schnitzler, Wasserman and Werfel, among others. Even Vienna produced little of importance in Hebrew. 'The great 30-year cultural period in Vienna – from 1890 to 1920 – did not coincide with a greater growth of Hebrew literature in the Austrian metropolis' (Silberschlag, 1985, p. 39).

6. A brief bibliography on empires and imperialism appears in the Bibliography.

CHAPTER 1

1. A fuller account of the impact of the Assyrian, Babylonian and Persian empires upon the kingdoms of Israel and Judah, with many extracts from the prophets

and bibliography, is given by Aberbach (1993a). The classic sociological analysis of the prophets is that of Weber (1952). For a sociological study of the ancient near eastern empires in the context of the history of power, see Mann (1986). A useful survey of sociological approaches to the study of the world of the prophets is by Mayes (1989).

CHAPTER 2

1. The moral duty recognized by the rabbis to reproduce verbatim the words of their teachers is stated in the Mishna: 'One is duty-bound to quote one's master verbatim' (*Eduyot* 1, 3). See the Introduction, note 3 above.
2. On literary responses to loss, see Aberbach (1989). Jewish literary depictions of catastrophe are discussed with exceptional insight by Mintz (1984) and Roskies (1984).
3. On the development of anti-Semitism from the Roman period to modern times, see Poliakov (1965–85). For anti-Semitic texts of the Roman period, see Stern (1974–84). Also see Gager (1983) and Whittaker (1984).
4. A similar story is related in *Mekhilta de-Rabbi Ishmael* (Lauterbach, 1933, II, pp. 193–4).
5. Chaim Raphael describes the change in the Jewish image after the war of 66–73 CE:

> The Sabbath and the Sabbatical Year of Release had long been comic ideas to the Romans, but after the bitterness of the Jewish war they began to make fun of these curious institutions not good-humouredly but with contempt. This development, shown clearly enough in the stories of the Midrash, can be seen equally well in the Latin writers. Horace and Ovid, before the war, laugh at the Jews good-humouredly, but Juvenal and Martial [after the war] find them detestable. The word 'Jew' is a sign of contempt. The Jews are dirty, stupid, servile, seditious, licentious, greedy; their religion – the Sabbath, circumcision, abstention from pork – is barbarous, anti-Roman and antisocial. Even a prostitute, the Midrash tells us, found it an unforgiveable insult to be told she looked like a Jewess.
>
> (1968, p. 33)

The passages by Juvenal and Martial are quoted in full by Whittaker (1984).
6. The literal translation of *yefashpesh be-ma'asav* is 'he should investigate his past deeds'; another reading is *yemashmesh be-ma'asav*, 'let him examine his future actions'.
7. Rabbi Simeon bar Yochai, who spent years in hiding from the Romans, is the author of the saying, 'The best of the *goyim* – kill!' (*Mekhilta Beshalakh* 2). Oral and written rabbinic literature included a strong current of resistance:

> The struggle of the Jewish people against Greek and Roman domination was accompanied by a literature which encouraged and intensified resistance. After military defeat it became frequently the only weapon, an important instrument of hope and survival.
>
> (Fischel, 1971, 8: 301).

The Torah itself became an instrument of resistance and separatism (*Berakhot* 61b – see p. 87 above), particularly the laws of purity and tithes which, Goodman (1983) writes, were *the* crucial characteristic of 2nd century *tannaic* Judaism: they set the Jews apart by emphasizing their role as a chosen people and focusing their memory on the Temple period and the vanished priesthood.

8. See variations on this aggadah in *Avodah Zarah* 2b. In assessing the historical value of aggadot such as these as well as *tannaic* halakhah, Goodman concludes that 'Stories about that time display a rare feel for history in what are mostly ahistorical writings... These rabbinic comments are those of close witnesses to the tragedy who show remarkable acquaintanceship with the tactics of Roman armies in quelling revolts' (1983, pp. 136, 137).

9. The wholesale replacement of a Jewish by a gentile population is described by Millar (1993) as 'the decisive transformation in the religious demography of the Holy Land in the Imperial period' (p. 348).

10. A similar story is found in Aesop's fables which some of the rabbis of the Roman period evidently knew.

11. *Pesikta de-Rab Kahana* II 4, edit. Buber, pp. 11b–12a; *Genesis Rabbah* 88, 4; *Leviticus Rabbah* 8, 1; *Numbers Rabbah* 3, 6.

12. Modern accounts often misleadingly emphasize elements in Roman philosophy, literature and law which point to the humanitarian treatment of slaves, or to the willing loyalty of some slaves to their masters. For a sociological analysis of slavery in the Roman empire, which stresses the viciousness of Roman slavery, its exploitation, cruelty and mutual hostility, see Hopkins (1978).

13. 'Scarcely a single territory governed by Rome could claim that anyone before the Romans had ever ruled them half as well as the Romans did. The outstanding, tragic exception was Judaea' (Grant, 1971, p. 221). So far as can be judged from the sources, gentiles in Palestine were not maltreated as Jews were: 'the non-Jewish population never had any extensive friction with the Roman authorities' (Mendels, 1992, p. 357).

14. See Heinemann and Gutmann (1971, 3: 95).

15. Gager (1983) expresses a similar view, arguing that the increasingly negative view of Judaism in the Roman empire of the 1st century CE was caused by the Great Revolt as well as the successes of Jewish proselytization:

> Roman officials were especially prone to enforce the restrictive side of their policy precisely because they saw Judaism as a persistent 'threat' among their own people... converts from an established religion [i.e. 'Romanism'] represent the worst possible threat to that religion.
>
> (p. 59)

On the irreconcilability of Roman religion and proselytizing Judaism, and the danger to Rome of mass conversion to Judaism, see M. Aberbach (1966, p. 40ff.) and Feldman (1993, p. 441). Epstein (1959, pp. 143–4) points out that the Jewish attitude to conversion was determined by the Noah laws.

For a selection of texts showing evidence of the attraction of Judaism in the Roman empire, see Whittaker (1984, pp. 85–91). Also see Feldman (1993) and Goodman (1994) for conflicting interpretations of these texts. The threat of ethical monotheism to the Roman empire after 135 CE did not, in fact, cease but continued more effectively and subversively via Christianity. Crone's observations on Roman attitudes to Christianity are pertinent to 1st century CE Judaism:

> What really made them [the Christians] dangerous was their capacity to unite hitherto disparate masses in the name of an alternative vision and thus, whether this was intended or not, create an alternative power structure which the emperors ultimately preferred to have on their side rather than against them.
>
> (1989, p. 72)

On Jewish nationalism in the context of other ancient nationalisms, see Smith (1991, p. 48ff.).

16. Also see Jerusalem Talmud, *Peah* I, 1, 15c, *Sotah* IX, 15 (16), 24c, and Tosefta *Avodah Zarah* I, 20: 'Rabbi Joshua was asked: Can a father teach his son Greek [Tosefta *Avodah Zarah*: a Greek book]? He replied: A father can – at a time which is neither day nor night.' In a revealing talmudic juxtaposition, the question whether the study of Greek is permitted or not is squeezed between discussions of two passages in the Mishna: 'It is wrong to breed pigs' and 'It is wrong to breed a dog unless kept on a chain' (*Bava Kamma* 82b–83a). Ideological opposition to Greek culture may be dated from the Hasmonean period and the attempt of the Syro-Hellenists in the 2nd century BCE to ban Judaism and impose Hellenism on the Judeans. 'Cursed the man who breeds pigs and cursed the man who teaches his son Greek wisdom' (*ibid.* 82b). The aversion to the Greeks and their ideas and customs was, in fact, not uncommon among Romans (Cato is perhaps the classic example). Juvenal, a contemporary of Rabbi Ishmael, attacks the Greeks:

> I cannot, citizens, stomach
> A Greek-struck Rome. Yet what fraction of these sweepings
> Derives, in fact from Greece? For years now Syrian
> Orontes has poured its sewerage into our native Tiber –
> Its lingo and manners, its flutes, its outlandish harps
> With their transverse strings, its native tambourines,
> And the whores who hang out round the race course.
>
> Satire III 61–67
> (1974, p. 89)

17. See M. Aberbach (1994) and the Introduction, pp. 15–16 above. For an attempt to distinguish the *tannaim* as an elite social group in contrast with the post-mishnaic rabbinic movement, see Cohen (1992).

18. Such concentration as that of Akiva was also a necessary feature of the new intricacies of talmudic discussion. In one amusing anecdote (which, however, has a tragic conclusion in the description of Akiva's death), Moses himself, the ultimate source of rabbinic authority, finds himself in Akiva's school. Not understanding a word, Moses is ignominiously banished to the back row as the worst pupil. However, when asked on whose authority he has based a particular halakhic ruling, Akiva replies: 'It was passed down to Moses at Sinai' (*Menahot* 29b). By the time of Akiva, Jewish law had gone so far beyond the teachings of Moses that the great lawgiver himself would no longer have been able to understand the numerous re-interpretations attributed to him.

19. Grant describes the Romans as 'the first nation to treat law in a scientific way' (1960, p. 81) and the Roman legal code as 'the greatest of Roman achievements, one of the outstanding creations of the human mind' (p. 82) and 'the most far-reaching of all Rome's contributions to posterity' (1978, p. 290).

20. Rabbi Eliezer ben Hyrkanus' spirit of dissent was expressed in his hate of gentiles (*Mekhilta* on Exodus 14:31; Passover Haggadah), in his alleged sympathy towards Christianity (Tosefta *Hullin* II 24; *Avodah Zarah* 16b–17a), and in his opposition to the standardization of prayer (Mishna *Berakhot* IV 4).

21. These are summed up by Schechter (1909): (a) the faith that the Messiah, a descendant of the house of David, will restore the kingdom of Israel, which under his sceptre will extend over the whole world; (b) the notion that a last terrible battle will take place with the enemies of God (or Israel), who will strive against the establishment of the kingdom, and who will finally be destroyed. 'When will the Lord be King for ever and ever? When the heathens – that is – the Romans – will have perished out of the land' (Midrash *Tehillim* 10, 7, edit. Buber, p. 96); (c) the belief that the establishment of this new kingdom will be followed by the spiritual hegemony of Israel, when all the nations will accept the belief in the unity of God, acknowledge his kingdom and seek instruction from his law; (d) the conviction that it will be an age of material happiness as well as spiritual bliss for all those who are included in the kingdom, when further death will disappear and the dead will revive (1975, p. 102).

22. See the Introduction above and the Conclusion of Chapter 2 below. The widespread use of Hebrew in Galilee in the post-135 CE period may be attributed in part at least to the successful efforts of the rabbis. For a survey of the language situation at the time, see Schürer (1979, II, pp. 20–8; 60–80) and a short summary by Goodman (1983, pp. 66–8). On the question why aggadah was primarily associated with the Land of Israel, see Shinan (1990, pp. 17–20).

23. According to Simkins (1987):

It would be an entirely distorted reading of history to believe that [the Roman soldiers] were very different from the peoples they subjugated. The Roman army created conditions in which for centuries on end, a farmer could normally hope to till his fields secure in the knowledge that a marauding band from a neighbouring tribe would not be permitted to carry off the fruit of his labour and probably to slaughter or enslave him and his family in the bargain. Under the *Pax Romana* a man could travel from Palmyra in Syria to Eburacum in north Britain without a passport and without ever feeling entirely out of place. Wherever he went, Rome had established a miniature version of the mother city, with markets, baths, temples and all the other complexities of the 'Roman way.' It was for the establishment of these benefits and the maintenance of that order that the Roman army was directly responsible.

(p. 26)

This assessment emphasizes the benefits brought by the Roman army while ignoring the lawless exactions, especially from the poor, perpetrated by Roman soldiers and officials. The Jews in Galilee had little reason to like the Roman army (Oppenheimer, 1992). Yet it is true to say that if not for the military might of the Roman empire, and the unity and stability which it enforced, the Mishna and much of the Midrash might never have been written.

24. The Messiah is mentioned only twice in the Mishna: *Berakhot* I 5; *Sotah* IX 15. This may have been precautionary because of the Romans but perhaps also because a Messiah would have put an end to the Patriarchal regime. See *Sanhedrin* 38a.

25. See Chapter 2, note 2 above.

26. Also see Jerusalem Talmud *Shabbat* I, 3, 3c.

27. On possible influences of Stoic philosophy on rabbinic literature, see Hengel (1981) and Abraham Wasserstein (1994). According to the latter, rabbinic Judaism and Christianity 'shared the basic moral and cosmic optimism of stoic thought which, through its translation to the Roman empire, had become one of the formative influences on the character of Europe' (p. 228). The contrary view – that on the basis of the available evidence it is doubtful whether Stoicism influenced the rabbis – is expressed, among others, by Feldman (1971, 1993).

28. On deviance amplification, see Wilkins (1964) and Ditton (1979). This concept suggests, among other things, that distorted information and ignorance about minorities in a mass society may spiral into ever-increasing significance through labelling and over-reaction. As applied to the Roman empire, it would imply that, especially after 70 CE, anti-Semitism in some ways stimulated an expansion of Jewish identity and a greater degree of individuality and originality in Judaism than would have been likely otherwise.

29. Millar (1993), pointing out that the Roman force arrayed against Jerusalem alone during the five-month siege of 70 CE represented roughly one-seventh of the entire imperial army, concludes:

'Nothing could have served to emphasize more clearly the degree to which the coherence of the Empire depended on at least passive acquiescence by the provincial population, or at the very least the absence of any coherent local or regional nationalism, which might offer a challenge to Rome.

(p. 76)

The triumph held in Rome in 71 CE to celebrate the Roman victory over Judaea was 'the only triumph ever to celebrate the subjugation of the population of an existing province' (*ibid.* p. 79). Similarly, the coins minted to commemorate the capture of Judaea have no parallel in Roman treatment of its provinces (Goodman, 1987, p. 235).

CHAPTER 3

1. Hebrew texts in this chapter are translated by David Aberbach from Schirmann (1959), unless indicated otherwise. Apart from Carmi (1981), recent bilingual selections of medieval Hebrew poetry include Scheindlin (1986, 1991). For a brief but comprehensive introduction to medieval Hebrew poetry by an important modern Hebrew poet, see Pagis (1971). Also, see Goldstein (1965) and Stillman (1979).

2. From a sociological viewpoint, Spain was unique in a number of other ways: in having been a Roman province, then later an undifferentiated province of Western Christianity, and in having undergone Germanic conquest, with the result that 'Even the Christians displayed a degree of assimilation that is scarcely paralleled in the east' (Crone and Cook, 1977, p. 115). On the extraordinary degree to which Arabic conventions entered Hebrew, see Schippers (1994).

3. According to Brann (1991):

> Abd ar-Rahman III's Umayyad predecessors repeatedly sought to exert Cordoba's centralizing authority over a territory and population torn by numerous tribal, ethnic, and social cleavages, socio-economic and religious struggles, and factional rivalries: Arabs battled with Berbers, Syrian Arabs quarreled with Yemenis, and Arab Muslims competed with native Iberian neo-Muslims and their descendants (Ar. *muwalladūn*). The *sagāliba* or 'Slavs', praetorian guards of diverse European origin, brought to Spain as slaves at a young age, were involved in revolts against Umayyad authority as well. Mozarabic Christians, not without considerable ambivalence, occasionally resisted the idea of living with an Islamic polity. Under such complex and unpredictably shifting political circumstances, it is easy to appreciate why the Jewish community, which had no stake in the various internecine disputes among Muslims and which could be neither accused of harbouring a subversive allegiance to any sovereign power nor suspected of entertaining an obligation to any anti-Umayyad cause, might have warranted the trust of the Umayyads.
>
> (p. 4)

The diversity in Muslim Spain was, at the same time, part of the wider unified Islamic empire, as David Wasserstein points out: 'It is precisely this pattern of regional disjunction within a broader context of fundamental social unity, as part of the universal society of Islam, which marks Iberian Islam from start to finish' (1985, p. 294).

4. The translation of this and the other Arabic verse quoted below has been revised by David Aberbach.

5. For a more detailed and convincing argument that the most original Arabic poetry was written in its earliest phase, in the 9th-11th centuries, see Giffen (1971).

6. *Malkah resha'ah* (Evil queen, i.e. Christian Spain) is apparently a play on *malkhut resha'ah* (evil empire) which in the Talmud (e.g. *Berakhot* 61b) describes Rome. See p. 55 above. The collected poems of Hanagid are edited by Jarden (1966).

7. The imagery and language here owe much to the book of Nahum. See pp. 38–9 above.

8. Jarden (1975, p. 333). Schirmann (1959, I, p. 231) has *lihyot* (to be) rather than *lihyot* (to live).

9. Schirmann (1959, I, p. 202) dates this poem 1039–40.

10. Schirmann (1959, I, p. 243) notes the biblical references in this poem: Genesis 16:12; 21:17; Psalms 80:14 with its gloss in *Leviticus Rabbah* 13, 'The pig is Edom' (i.e. Rome).

11. For a literary study of Ibn Ezra's poetry, see Pagis (1970).

12. See, for example, Schirmann (1959, I, pp. 386, 460), where Halevi describes Andalusia in biblical language reminiscent of his poems of Zion. Halevi's hope that messianic redemption from what he describes as arrogant and oppressive Muslim rule would occur in 1130 is expressed in the poem beginning *Namta venirdamta* (*ibid.*, p. 480).

13. On the artistic problems inherent in being a Hebrew poet in Muslim Spain, see Brann (1991).

CHAPTER 4

1. Mostly because it asserted Jewish national distinctiveness, Hebrew was banned under Soviet rule; and it is highly significant that many leading Soviet dissidents in the 1970s and 1980s, such as Scharansky, were teachers and students of Hebrew.

2. On Mendele and his milieu, with literary and historical bibliography, see Aberbach (1993). The most comprehensive recent history of Hebrew literature of the period 1881–1917 is Shaked's (1977).

3. Sholom Aleichem: Hebrew 'How do you do?' Pen name of Sholom Rabinowitz.

4. Ahad Ha'am: Hebrew 'One of the people', pen name of Asher Ginsberg. On Ahad Ha'am's rivalry with Herzl, see Zipperstein (1993).

5. Only one other major Hebrew writer – Agnon – followed Mendele in this ambivalent, satiric mode of depiction of European Jews, which became the essence of his style (Aberbach, 1984, 1994). But in contrast with Mendele a generation earlier, Agnon was totally committed to Zionism, and he wrote most of his works in Jerusalem.

6. Gogol's claim to love Russia seems to have been true for the most part when he was out of the country (which he was while writing *Dead Souls*). When he lived in Russia, he appears to have despised it (Maguire, 1994, pp. 176–7).

Bibliography

I. GENERAL

Aberbach, David (1981). 'On re-reading Bialik: Paradoxes of a "National Poet",' *Encounter* 56, 6: 41–8.

Aberbach, David (1984). *At the Handles of the Lock: Themes in the Fiction of S.J. Agnon.* Oxford University Press, Littman Library.

Aberbach, David (1988). *Bialik.* Jewish Thinkers series. London: Peter Halban; New York: Grove Press. Hebrew edition, Jerusalem: Eked/Yediot, 1992.

Aberbach, David (1989). *Surviving Trauma: loss, literature and psychoanalysis.* New Haven, Conn.: Yale University Press.

Aberbach, David (1993). *Realism, Caricature and Bias: the Fiction of Mendele Mocher Sefarim.* Oxford: Littman Library.

Aberbach, David, (1993a). *Imperialism and Biblical Prophecy 750–500 BCE.* London: Routledge.

Aberbach, David (1994). 'Fantasies of Deviance in Mendele and Agnon.' *AJS Review* XIX, 1: 45–60.

Aberbach, David (1995). 'Aggadah and Childhood Imagination in the Works of Mendele, Bialik and Agnon.' In *Jewish Education and Learning,* G. Abramson and T. Parfitt (eds). Festschrift for David Patterson. Chur, Switzerland: Harwood Academic Publications.

Aberbach, David (1995a). *Hebrew Poetry, Jewish Nationalism and the Empire of Islam 1031–1140.* London: London School of Economics.

Aberbach, David (1996). 'Charisma in Politics, Religion and the Media: Private Trauma, Public Ideals'. London: Macmillan.

Aberbach, David (1997). 'Revolutionary Hebrew, Empire and Crisis: Toward a Sociological *Gestalt.*' *British Journal of Sociology,* 48, 1: 131–51.

Aberbach, David (1997a). 'The Iron Age, Imperialism and Biblical Prophecy.' *Israel Affairs,* 4, 1.

Aberbach, David (1997b). 'Hebrew Literature and Jewish Nationalism in the Tsarist Empire 1881–1917.' *Nations and Nationalism,* 3, 1: 25–44.

Aberbach, David (1997c), 'Defeat and Cultural Nationalism: Hebrew Creativity in the Roman Empire 66–200 CE.' London: London School of Economics.

Aberbach, Moses (1966). *The Roman–Jewish War 66–70 CE.* London: The Jewish Quarterly.

Aberbach, Moshe (1985). *Jewish Education in the Time of the Mishna and Talmud* (Hebrew). Jerusalem: Reuben Mass.

Aberbach, Moshe (1994). *Labor, Crafts and Commerce in Ancient Israel.* Jerusalem: The Magnes Press, The Hebrew University.

Abramson, Glenda (ed.) (1996). *The Oxford Book of Hebrew Short Stories.* Oxford University Press.

Ahad Ha'am (1965). *Collected Works* (Hebrew). Jerusalem: Hotzaah Ivrit; Tel Aviv: Dvir.

Alon, Gedalia (1977). *Jews, Judaism and the Classical World.* Trans. I. Abrahams. Jerusalem: The Magnes Press, The Hebrew University.

Alon, Gedalia (1980). *The Jews in Their Land in the Talmudic Age (70–640 C.E.)*. 2 vols. Trans. and ed. G. Levi. Jerusalem: The Magnes Press, The Hebrew University.

Alter, Robert (1975). *Modern Hebrew Literature*. New York: Behrman House.

Alter, Robert (1988). *The Invention of Hebrew Prose: Modern Fiction and the Language of Realism*. Seattle: Washington University Press.

Arberry, A.J. (1965). *Arabic Poetry: A Primer for Students*. Cambridge University Press.

Ashtor, Eliyahu (1973, 1979, 1984). *The Jews of Moslem Spain*. 3 vols. Trans. from the Hebrew by A. Klein and J.M. Klein. Philadelphia: Jewish Publication Society.

Aurelius, Marcus (1992; orig. 1946 and 2nd century CE). *Meditations*. Trans. A.S.L. Farquharson. London: Everyman.

Avi-Yonah, Michael (1976). *The Jews of Palestine: A Political History from the Bar-Kokhba War to the Arab Conquest*. Oxford: Basil Blackwell.

Baron, Salo (1952–). *A Social and Religious History of the Jews*. 17 vols. New York: Columbia University Press.

Baron, Salo (1971), 'Population,' *Encyclopedia Judaica* 13: 866–903.

Belinsky, Vissarion (1981). *Selected Philosophical Works*, Westport, Conn.: Hyperion Press.

Ben-Yehuda, Eliezer (1983; orig. 1917–18). *A Dream Come True*. Trans. T. Muraoko, ed. G. Mandel. Modern Hebrew Classics. Oxford: Westview Press.

Bialik, Chaim Nachman, and Ravnitsky, Yehoshua Hana (eds) (1992; orig. 1908–11). *The Book of Legends (Sefer Ha-Aggadah)*. Trans. W.G. Braude. New York: Schocken Books.

Brann, Ross (1991). *The Compunctious Poet: Cultural Ambiguity and Hebrew Poetry in Muslim Spain*. Baltimore, Md. and London: Johns Hopkins University Press.

Carmi, T. (ed.) (1981). *The Penguin Book of Hebrew Verse*. New York: Viking; Harmondsworth, Middlesex: Penguin Books.

Chekhov, Anton (1978; orig. 1904). *The Cherry Orchard*. Trans. M. Frayn. London: Methuen.

Cohen, Shaye J.D. (1992). 'The Place of the Rabbi in Jewish Society of the Second Century.' In Lee. I. Levine, ed., *The Galilee in Late Antiquity*. New York and Jerusalem: Jewish Theological Seminary of America.

Crone, Patricia (1989). *Pre-Industrial Society*. Oxford: Blackwell.

Crone, Patricia and Cook, Michael (1977). *Hagarism: The Making of the Islamic World*. Cambridge University Press.

Daube, David (1949). 'Rabbinic Methods of Interpretation and Hellenistic Rhetoric.' In *Collected Works of David Daube*, vol. 1 (1992): *Talmudic Law*. Ed. C. Carmichael. Robbins Collection Publication: University of California at Berkeley.

Davidson, Israel (1966; orig. 1907). *Parody in Jewish Literature*, New York: AMS Press.

Ditton, Jason (1979). *Contrology: Beyond the New Criminality*. London. Macmillan.

Dostoevsky, Fyodor (1952; orig. 1871–2). *The Possessed (The Devils)*. 2 vols. Trans. C. Garnett. London: Dent.

Dostoevsky, Fyodor (1966; orig. 1865–6). *Crime and Punishment*. Trans. D. Magarshak. Harmondsworth, Middlesex: Penguin.

Dostoevsky, Fyodor (1978; orig. 1878–80). *The Brothers Karamazov*. 2 vols. Trans. D. Magarshak. Harmondsworth, Middlesex: Penguin Books.

Dostoevsky, Fyodor (1987). *Selected Letters*. Eds J. Frank and D.I. Goldstein; trans. A.R. MacAndrew. New Brunswick, NJ and London: Rutgers University Press.

Dostoevsky, Fyodor (1995; orig. 1860). *The House of the Dead*. Trans. D. McDuff. Harmondsworth, Middlesex: Penguin.

Duff, A.M. (1957). *Freedmen in the Early Roman Empire*. Cambridge: W. Heffer.

Dyson, Stephen L. (1971). 'Native revolts in the Roman empire.' *Historia* 20: 239–74.

Eliot, T.S. (1951). *Selected Essays*. London: Faber.

Ellmann, Richard (1968). *The Identity of Yeats*. London: Faber.

Epstein, Isidor (1959). *Judaism*. Harmondsworth, Middlesex: Penguin Books.

Erikson, Erik (1974) *Identity: Youth and Crisis*. London: Faber.

Ezra, Moses Ibn. *Shire ha-Hol* (Secular Poems): vol. I, ed. H. Brody, Berlin and Jerusalem: Schocken, 1934; vol. II, ed. H. Brody, Jerusalem: Schocken, 1942; vol. III, ed. D. Pagis, Jerusalem: Schocken, 1977.

Feierberg, Mordecai Zvi (1978). *Whither? and other stories*. Trans. H. Halkin. Philadelphia: Jewish Publication Society.

Feldman, Louis H. (1971). 'Hellenism and the Jews.' *Encyclopedia Judaica* 8: 295–301, s.v. 'Hellenism'.

Feldman, Louis H. (1993). *Jew and Gentile in the Ancient World: Attitudes and Interaction from Alexander to Justinian*. Princeton, NJ: Princeton University Press.

Fischel, Henry Albert (1971). 'Spiritual resistance.' *Encyclopedia Judaica* 8: 301–3, s.v. 'Hellenism'.

Fishman, J.A. (ed.) (1985). *Readings in the Sociology of Jewish Languages*. Leiden: E.J. Brill.

Fleischer, Ezra (1971). '*Piyyut*.' *Encyclopedia Judaica* 13: 573–602.

Fox, Robin Lane (1986). *Pagans and Christians*. Harmondsworth, Middlesex: Penguin Books.

Frankel, Jonathan (1981). *Prophecy and Politics: Socialism, Nationalism, and the Russian Jews, 1862–1917*. Cambridge University Press.

Fuller, William C. (1985). *Civil-Military Conflict in Imperial Russia 1881–1914*. Princeton, NJ: Princeton University Press.

Gager, John G. (1983). *The Origins of Anti-Semitism: Attitudes toward Judaism in Pagan and Christian Antiquity*. New York and Oxford: Oxford University Press.

Gibbon, Edward (1960; orig. 1776, 1781, 1788). *The Decline and Fall of the Roman Empire*. 1 vol. abridgement. Ed. D.M. Low. New York: Harcourt, Brace.

Giffen, Lois Anita (1971). *Theory of Profane Love Among the Arabs: The Development of the Genre*. New York: New York University Press; London: London University Press.

Glick, Thomas (1979). *Islamic and Christian Spain in the Early Middle Ages*. Princeton, NJ: Princeton University Press.

Gogol, Nikolai (1976; orig. 1842). *Dead Souls*. Trans. D. Magarshak. Harmondsworth, Middlesex: Penguin Classics.

Goldmann, Lucien (1964; orig. 1956). *The Hidden God: A Study of Tragic Vision in the Pensées of Pascal and the Tragedies of Racine*. Trans. P. Thody. London: Routledge & Kegan Paul.

Goldstein, David I. (1981; orig. 1976). *Dostoyevsky and the Jews*. Austin, Texas. and London: University of Texas Press.

Goodman, Martin (1983). *State and Society in Roman Galilee, A.D. 132–212*. Totowa, NJ: Rowman & Allanheld.

Goodman, Martin (1987). *The Ruling Class of Judaea: The Origins of the Jewish Revolt Against Rome A.D. 66–70*. Cambridge University Press.

Goodman, Martin (1994). *Mission and Conversion: Proselytizing in the Religious History of the Roman Empire.* Oxford University Press.

Goodman, Martin (1996). 'Judaea.' In A.K. Bowman, E. Champlin and A. Lintott (eds), *Cambridge Ancient History*, vol. X, 2nd edn, *The Augustan Empire, 43 B.C.–A.D. 69.* Cambridge University Press.

Goodman, Martin (forthcoming). 'Judaea'. In A.K. Bowman, P. Garnsey, D. Rathbone, eds, *Cambridge Ancient History*, vol. XI, 2nd edn. Cambridge University Press.

Grant, Michael (1960). *The World of Rome.* London: Weidenfeld & Nicolson.

Grant, Michael (1971). *Herod the Great.* New York: American Heritage Press.

Grant, Michael (1978). *History of Rome.* London: Weidenfeld & Nicolson.

Haberer, Erich E. (1995). *Jews and Revolution in Nineteenth-Century Russia.* Cambridge University Press.

Hall, John. (1979). *The Sociology of Literature,* London and New York: Longman.

Hartman, Geoffrey and Budick, Sanford (eds) (1986). *Midrash and Literature.* New Haven, Conn. and London: Yale University Press.

Heinemann, Joseph and Gutmann, Joshua (1971). 'Anti-Semitism.' *Encyclopedia Judaica* 3: 87–96.

Hengel, Martin (1981; orig. 1973). *Judaism and Hellenism: Studies in their Encounter in Palestine during the Early Hellenistic Period.* 2 vols. Trans. J. Bowden. London: SCM Press.

Hopkins, Keith (1978). *Conquerors and Slaves.* Cambridge University Press.

Hourani, Albert (1991). *A History of the Arab Peoples.* London: Faber.

Hroch, Miroslav (1985). *Social Preconditions of National Revival in Europe.* Cambridge University Press.

Hutchinson, John (1987). *The Dynamics of Cultural Nationalism.* London: Allen & Unwin.

Jacobs, Louis (1984). *The Talmudic Argument: A study in Talmudic reasoning and methodology.* Cambridge University Press.

Jarden, Dov (ed.) (1966). *Divan Shmuel Hanagid* (Hebrew). Jerusalem: Hebrew Union College Press.

Jarden, Dov (ed.) (1975). *The Secular Poetry of Rabbi Solomon Ibn Gabirol* (Hebrew). Jerusalem: Kiryat Noar.

Jenkyns, Richard (ed.) (1992). *The Legacy of Rome.* Oxford University Press.

Juvenal (1974; orig. 1967). *The Sixteen Satires.* Trans. P. Green. Harmondsworth, Middlesex: Penguin.

Kaufmann, Yehezkel (1970). *History of the Religion of Israel,* vol. IV: *The Babylonian Captivity and Deutero-Isaiah.* Trans. M. Greenberg. New York: Union of American Hebrew Congregations.

Kedourie, Elie (1960). *Nationalism.* London: Hutchinson.

Klier, John D. (1995). *Imperial Russia's Jewish Question, 1855–1881.* Cambridge University Press.

Klier, John D. and Lambroza, Shlomo (eds) (1992). *Pogroms: Anti-Jewish Violence in Modern Russian History.* Cambridge University Press.

de Lange, Nicholas (1987). *Judaism.* New York and Oxford: Oxford University Press.

Latourette, Kenneth Scott (1938–47). *A History of the Expansion of Christianity.* 7 vols. London: Eyre & Spottiswoode.

Laurenson, Diana and Swingewood, Alan (1972). *The Sociology of Literature.* London: MacGibbon & Kee.

Lederhendler, Eli (1989). *The Road to Modern Jewish Politics: Political Tradition and Political Reconstruction in the Jewish Community of Tsarist Russia.* New York and Oxford: Oxford University Press.

Levin, Gabriel (1992). 'Yehuda Halevi and Moshe Ibn Ezra.' *Ariel* 87: 35–6.

Levine, Lee I. (1989). *The Rabbinic Class of Roman Palestine in Late Antiquity.* Jerusalem and New York: Yad Itzhak Ben-Zvi and The Jewish Theological Seminary of America.

Lewis, Bernard (1984). *The Jews of Islam,* London: Routledge.

Lieberman, Saul (1950). *Hellenism in Jewish Palestine: studies in the literary transmission, beliefs and manners of Palestine in the I century B.C.E. – IV century C.E.* New York: Jewish Theological Seminary of America.

Lieberman, Saul (1963). 'How Much Greek in Jewish Palestine?' In *Studies and Texts,* vol. 1: *Biblical and Other Studies,* ed. A. Altmann. Cambridge, Mass.: Harvard University Press.

Löwe, Heinz-Dietrich (1993). *The Tsars and the Jews: Reform, Reaction and Anti-Semitism in Imperial Russia, 1772–1917.* Chur, Switzerland: Harwood Academic Publishers.

Maccoby, Hyam (1988). *Early Rabbinic Writings.* Cambridge University Press.

MacMullen, Ramsay (1988). *Corruption and the Decline of Rome.* New Haven, Conn.: Yale University Press.

Maguire, Robert A. (1994). *Exploring Gogol.* Stanford, Calif.: Stanford University Press.

Mann, Michael (1986). *The Sources of Social Power: A History of Power from the Beginning to A.D. 1760.* Vol. 1. Cambridge University Press.

Marx, Karl (1845–6). 'The German Ideology.' In *The Marx-Engels Reader.* Ed. R.C. Tucker. New York: W.W. Norton, 1972.

Mayes, A.D.H. (1989). 'Sociology and the Old Testament.' In R.E. Clements (ed.), *The World of Ancient Israel: Sociological, anthropological and political perspectives.* Cambridge University Press.

Mekhilta de-Rabbi Ishmael (1933; orig. 2nd c. CE). Ed. J.Z. Lauterbach. 3 vols. Philadelphia: Jewish Publication Society.

Mendele Mocher Sefarim (1947) *Collected Works of Mendele Mocher Sefarim* (Hebrew). 1 vol. edn. Tel Aviv: Dvir.

Mendele Mocher Sefarim (1949; orig. 1878). *The Travels of Benjamin the Third.* Trans. M. Spiegel, New York: Schocken Books.

Mendels, Doron (1992). *The Rise and Fall of Jewish Nationalism.* New York: Doubleday.

Mendes-Flohr, Paul R. and Reinharz, Judah (eds) (1980). *The Jew in the Modern World: A Documentary History.* New York and Oxford: Oxford University Press.

Meyers, Eric M. (1992). 'Roman Sephoris in Light of New Archaeological Evidence'. In Lee I. Levine, ed. *The Galilee in Late Antiquity.* New York and Jerusalem: The Jewish Theological Seminary of America.

Millar, Fergus (1993). *The Roman Near East 31 BC – AD 337.* Cambridge, Mass.: Harvard University Press.

Mintz, Alan (1984). *Hurban: Response to Catastrophe in Hebrew Literature.* New York: Columbia University Press.

Mintz, Alan (1989). *Banished From Their Father's Table: loss of faith and Hebrew autobiography.* Bloomington: Indiana University Press.

Miron, Dan (1987). *When Loners Come Together: A Portrait of Hebrew Literature at the Turn of the Twentieth Century* (Hebrew). Tel Aviv: Am Oved.

Monroe, James T. (ed.) (1974). *Hispano-Arabic Poetry: A Student Anthology.* Berkeley and Los Angeles: University of California Press.

Neusner, Jacob (1987). *Vanquished Nation, Broken Spirit: The Virtues of the Heart in Formative Judaism.* Cambridge University Press.

Neusner, Jacob (ed.) (1988). *The Mishna: A New Translation.* New Haven, Conn. and London: Yale University Press.

Oppenheimer, Aharon (1992). 'Roman Rule and the Cities of the Galilee in Talmudic Literature'. In Lee. I. Levine, ed., *The Galilee in Late Antiquity.* New York and Jerusalem: The Jewish Theologica; Seminary of America.

Pagis, Dan (1970). *Secular Poetry and Poetic Theory: Moses Ibn Ezra and His Contemporaries* (Hebrew). Jerusalem: Mossad Bialik.

Pagis, Dan (1971). 'Medieval Hebrew Secular Poetry.' *Encyclopedia Judaica* 13: 681–690, s.v. 'Poetry'.

Patterson, David (1964). *The Hebrew Novel in Tsarist Russia.* Edinburgh University Press.

Patterson, David (1985). 'The Influence of Hebrew Literature on the Growth of Jewish Nationalism in the Nineteenth Century.' In R. Sussex and J. C. Eade (eds), *Culture and Nationalism in Nineteenth-Century Eastern Europe.* Columbus, Ohio: Slavica Publishers.

Patterson, David (1985a). 'Moving Centers in Modern Hebrew Literature.' In *The Great Transition: The Recovery of the Lost Centers of Modern Hebrew Literature.* Eds G. Abramson and T. Parfitt. Totowa, NJ: Rowman & Allanheld.

Pesikta de-Rab Kahana (1975). Trans. W.G. Braude and I. J. Kapstein. Philadelphia: Jewish Publication Society.

Petuchowski, Jakob J. (1978). *Theology and Poetry: Studies in the Medieval Piyyut.* London: Routledge & Kegan Paul.

Pipes, Richard (1990). *The Russian Revolution 1899–1919.* London: Collins Harvill.

Poliakov, Leon (1965–85). *The History of Anti-Semitism.* 4 vols. Trans. R. Howard et al. New York: Vanguard Press.

Pritchard, James B., ed. (1969). *Ancient Near Eastern Texts Relating to the Old Testament,* 3rd edn. Princeton, NJ: Princeton University Press.

Raphael, Chaim (1968). *The Walls of Jerusalem: An Excursion Into Jewish History.* London: Chatto & Windus.

Reif, Stefan C. (1993). *Judaism and Hebrew Prayer: New perspectives on Jewish liturgical history.* Cambridge University Press.

Rogger, Hans (1986). *Jewish Politics and Right-Wing Politics in Imperial Russia.* London: Macmillan.

Roskies, David (1984). *Against the Apocalypse.* Cambridge, Mass.: Harvard University Press.

Sáenz-Badillos, Angel (1993). *A History of the Hebrew Language.* Trans. J. Elwolde. Cambridge University Press.

Saltykov-Shchedrin, Mikhail (1986; orig. 1875–80). *The Golovlets.* Trans. I. P. Foote. New York: Oxford University Press.

Schechter, Solomon (1975, orig. 1909). *Aspects of Rabbinic Theology.* New York: Schocken Books

Scheindlin, Raymond P. (1986). *Wine, Women, and Death: Medieval Hebrew Poems on the Good Life.* Philadelphia: Jewish Publication Society.

Scheindlin, Raymond P. (1991). *The Gazelle: Medieval Hebrew Poems on Israel, and the Soul.* Philadelphia and New York: Jewish Publication Society.

Schippers, Arie (1994). *Spanish-Hebrew Poetry and the Arabic Literary Tradition: Arabic Themes in Hebrew Andalusian Poetry.* Leiden: E. J. Brill.

Schirmann, Chaim (ed.) (1959). *Hebrew Poetry in Spain and Provence* (Hebrew) 3rd edn. 2 books in 4 parts. Jerusalem: Mossad Bialik; Tel Aviv: Dvir.

Schürer, Emil. *The History of the Jewish People in the Age of Jesus Christ (175 B.C. – A.D. 135):* Vol. I, eds G. Vermes and F. Millar, 1973; vol. II, eds G. Vermes, F. Millar and M. Black, 1979; vol. III, eds G. Vermes, F. Millar and M. Goodman, 1986, 1987. Edinburgh: T. & T. Clark.

Seltzer, Robert (1980). *Jewish People, Jewish Thought: the Jewish experience in history.* New York: Macmillan.

Shaked, Gershon (1977). *Hebrew Narrative 1880–1970* (Hebrew). Vol. 1. Tel Aviv: Hakibbutz Hame'uchad.

Shinan, Avigdor (1990). *The World of the Aggadah.* Trans. J. Glucker. Tel Aviv: MOD Books.

Sifre: A Tannaitic Commentary on the Book of Deuteronomy (1986; orig. 2nd century CE). Ed. and trans. R. Hammer. New Haven, Conn. and London: Yale University Press.

Silberschlag, Eisig (1985). 'Hebrew Literature in Vienna 1782–1939.' In G. Abramson and T. Parfitt (eds), *The Great Transition: The Recovery of Lost Centres of Modern Hebrew Literature.* Totowa, NJ: Rowman & Allanheld.

Simkins, Michael (1987). *The Roman Army from Caesar to Trajan.* Men-At-Arms series. London: Osprey.

Smallwood, E. Mary (1976). *The Jews under Roman Rule: From Pompey to Diocletian.* Leiden: E.J. Brill.

Smith, Anthony D. (1991). *National Identity.* Harmondsworth, Middlesex: Penguin.

Stanislawski, Michael (1988). *'For Whom Do I Toil?' J.L. Gordon and the Crisis of Russian Jewry.* New York: Oxford University Press.

Stanley, Brian (1990). *The Bible and the Flag: Protestant missions and British imperialism in the nineteenth and twentieth centuries.* Leicester: Appollos.

Stemberger, Günter (1996). *Introduction to the Talmud and Midrash.* 2nd edn. Trans. M. Bockmuel. Edinburgh: T. & T. Clark. Revision of H. L. Strack, *Introduction to the Talmud* (1887).

Stern Menahem (1974–84). *Greek and Latin Authors on Jews and Judaism.* 3 vols. Jerusalem: Israel Academy of Sciences and Humanities.

Stillman, Norman (1979). *The Jews of Arab Lands: A History and Source Book.* Philadelphia: Jewish Publication Society.

Tacitus (1992; orig. 1964). *The Histories.* Trans. K. Wellesley. Harmondsworth, Middlesex: Penguin Classics.

Tacitus (1989; orig. 1956). *The Annals of Imperial Rome.* Trans. M. Grant. Harmondsworth, Middlesex: Penguin Classics.

Tolstoy, Leo (1968; orig. 1874–6). *Anna Karenina.* Trans. R. Edmonds. Harmondsworth, Middlesex: Penguin.

Treadgold, Donald W. (1973). *The West in Russia and China.* Vol. 1: *Russia, 1472–1917.* Cambridge University Press.

Turgenev, Ivan (1965; orig. 1861). *Fathers and Sons.* Trans. R. Edmonds. Harmondsworth, Middlesex: Penguin.

Virgil (1959; orig. 1st c. CE). *The Aeneid.* Trans. W.F. Jackson Knight. Harmondsworth, Middlesex: Penguin Classics.

Vital, David (1975). *The Origins of Zionism.* New York and Oxford: Oxford University Press.

Wallach, Luitpold (1940–1). 'The Colloquy of Marcus Aurelius with the Patriarch Judah I.' *JOR* 31: 259–86.

Ward-Perkins, John (1977). *Roman Architecture*. New York: Harry N. Abrams.

Wasserstein, Abraham (1994). 'Greek Language and Philosophy.' In G. Abramson and T. Parfitt (eds), *Jewish Education and Learning (Festschrift* for David Patterson). Chur, Switzerland: Harwood Academic Publishers, pp. 221–31.

Wasserstein, David (1985). *The Rise and Fall of the Party-Kings: Politics and Society in Islamic Spain 1002–1086*. Princeton, NJ: Princeton University Press.

Watt, W. Montgomery (1984; orig. 1974). *The Majesty that Was Islam*. London: Sidgwick & Jackson.

Weber, Max (1952; orig. 1917–19). *Ancient Judaism*. Trans. and ed. H.H. Gerth and D. Martingale. New York: Free Press.

Weber, Max (1961; orig. 1923). *General Economic History*. Trans. F. H. Knight. New York: Collier Books.

Whittaker, Molly (1984). *Jews and Christians: Graeco-Roman Views*. Cambridge University Press.

Wilkins, Leslie T. (1964). *Social Deviance; Social Policy, Action and Research*. London: Tavistock.

Yadin, Yigael (1963). *The Art of Warfare in Biblical Lands in the Light of Archaeological Study*. 2 vols. New York: McGraw–Hill.

Yadin, Yigael (1971). *Bar-Kokhba*. New York: Random House; London: Weidenfeld & Nicolson.

Zinberg, Israel (1929–37). *A History of Jewish Literature*. 12 vols. Trans. and ed. B. Martin. Vols I–II, Philadelphia: Jewish Publication Society of America, 1972–3; vol. III, Cleveland and London: The Press of Case Western Reserve University, 1973; vols IV–XII, Cincinnati, Ohio: Hebrew Union College Press; New York: Ktav Publishing House, 1974–8.

Zipperstein, Steven J. (1985). *The Jews of Odessa: A Cultural History, 1794–1881*. Stanford, Calif.: Stanford University Press.

Zipperstein, Steven J. (1993). *Elusive Prophet: Ahad Ha'am and the Origins of Zionism*. London: Peter Halban.

II. EMPIRES AND IMPERIALISM

This list gives no more than a rough idea of some of the main authors, texts and currents of thought. There is virtually nothing on the impact of imperialism on Hebrew, David Aberbach's *Imperialism and Biblical Prophecy 750–500 BCE*, in the Bibliography above, gives a somewhat fuller list.

Doyle, Michael W. (1986). *Empires*. Ithaca, NY: Cornell University Press.

Garnsey, P.D.A. and Whittaker, C.R. (eds) (1978). *Imperialism in the Ancient World*. Cambridge University Press.

Harris, William V. (1985). *War and Imperialism in Republican Rome 327–70 B.C.* Oxford: Clarendon Press.

Hobson, J. (1938; orig. 1902). *Imperialism: A Study*. London: Allen & Unwin.

Lichtheim, George (1971). *Imperialism.* Harmondsworth, Middlesex: Penguin Books.

Mommsen, Wolfgang J. (1980). *Theories of Imperialism.* London: Weidenfeld & Nicolson.

Owen, R. and Sutcliffe, B. (eds) (1972). *Studies in the Theory of Imperialism.* London: Longman.

Schumpeter, Joseph A. (1951). *Imperialism and Social Classes.* Trans. H. Norden; ed. P.M. Sweezy. Oxford: Blackwell.

Index

Part 1. Hebrew
For individual writers, see the General Index

Part 2. General